Screwing
Around
With
Sex

Screwing Around With Sex:

Essays, Indictments, Anecdotes, and Asides

Paul R. Abramson

Asylum 4 Renegades Press
Joshua Tree, California

ASYLUM 4 RENEGADES PRESS
Joshua Tree, California
asylum4renegadespress.com

A4R seeks daring projects of interest to academic and educated readers. A4R admires risk-taking authors who write with intelligence and grace while remaining self-effacing and wryly humorous.

Paul R. Abramson
abramsonuclapsych.com

Cover Art and Book Design
Tania Love Abramson

First Edition

Praise for

SCREWING AROUND WITH SEX

I have, at times, insisted that the lives of sex researchers are pretty boring. Paul Abramson's collection of analytical essays, Screwing Around With Sex, *reveals that this is not always the case. Drawing on personal experiences and preoccupations necessitated by decades of scholarly investigation of sexuality, Abramson highlights the uneasy and sometimes painful interface of sexuality with our current moral landscape. In doing so, he elucidates the contradictions and complexities of contemporary sexuality in ways that frustrate, challenge, and inspire us to question our preconceived notions of what sexuality is—or should be.*

—Dr. Terri Conley, Professor of Psychology and Women's Studies, University of Michigan

The mix of effective anecdotes with the process of grappling with moral/scientific issues is very compelling. Chapter 3 ("On the Precipice of Porn") reminded me of David Foster Wallace's book Consider the Lobster, *in particular, Wallace's first chapter on the adult video industry.*

—Dr. Keith Holyoak, Distinguished Professor of Psychology, UCLA, and Editor of *Psychological Review*

Professor Abramson has made issues that are difficult, ancient, and current accessible without oversimplifying; urgent policy challenges tractable; and profound experiences understandable. Over and over as you read, you think, "Yes, we need to act."

—Dr. Gregory A. Miller, Distinguished Professor and Chair, Department of Psychology, UCLA

An idiosyncratic page-turner of a personal and professional journey that brought Paul Abramson to the heart of some of the most interesting issues of sexuality and sexual abuse in the late twentieth century and—through his role as a psychology professor serving as an expert witness—to the back stage of some of the nation's most important obscenity cases. Enjoyable and illuminating.

—Catherine Ross, Professor of Law, George Washington University Law School

6

Praise for Previous Books by
PAUL R. ABRAMSON

Abramson, P. R. (2010). *Sex Appeal: Six Ethical Principles for the 21st Century.* **New York, NY: Oxford University Press.**

What a great idea. . . . I completely agree with Abramson. . . . I do wish that more literature on the subject resembled [his] book.
— The New Yorker

*Very interesting . . . so interesting I may have to do multiple posts about it. So interesting that I was pissed when I just spilled coffee on it, because this is one book I plan to keep. . . . [In fact,] we could start a sexual revolution right here, through this blog, with help from **this** book.*
— Marie Claire

Sex Appeal *is the beginning of a conversation that has been a long time coming. How can people make safe, ethical choices about sex without sacrificing the fun of it? How can these* *choices make our lives, and the world, a better place? Paul Abramson explores these questions and more with six key concepts that will help readers to better understand how to prevent sexual harm while safely enjoying all of the benefits sex has to offer.* **Sex Appeal** *is provocative and refreshing in its embrace of a kind of sexual freedom that is at once both joyful and thoughtful.*

—**Dr. Ruth Westheimer (Dr. Ruth)**

[**Sex Appeal**] *is really smart, interesting, and honest.*

—**Nathan Schiller, Editor, *Construction Literary Magazine***

While it's unlikely to happen, [**Sex Appeal**] *should probably be part of the curriculum of every high school sex ed class. . . . [T]o a young person, the insights (or at least the lessons attached to them) could be huge.*

—*Feminist Review*

[Dr.] Abramson, an American professor of psychology and one of the most famous scholars of human sexuality, reminds us that the body is marching to the rhythm of the brain.

—*Le Regole Dell'Attrazione Magazine* **(Italy)**

Abramson, P. R. (2007). *Romance in the Ivory Tower: The Rights and Liberty of Conscience.* **Cambridge, MA: MIT Press.**

Make no mistake—Paul Abramson's book is a serious and thought-provoking examination of the extent to which institutions should proscribe individual actions. Although I do not endorse all of the conclusions, I strongly recommend this book.

—Lord Robert May, Oxford University

Romance in the Ivory Tower *presents a compelling argument about the erosion of the rights of privacy and conscience. The debate in this book transcends the issue of personal relationships within academia and engages fundamental questions of liberty and personal choice.*

—Nadine Strossen, President, American Civil Liberties Union

Abramson, P. R., Pinkerton, S. D., & Huppin, M. (2003). *Sexual Rights in America: The Ninth Amendment and the Pursuit of Happiness.* New York: NYU Press.

This frank and lucid book peels the fig leaf off various forms of legal regulation of sexuality and argues with passion and rich historical detail that individuals should have strong autonomy over their sexual expression as long as their sexual relationships are grounded in consent. The authors' comprehensive approach makes a considerable contribution to the literature.

—**Kathleen Sullivan, Dean, Stanford Law School**

Abramson, P. R., & Pinkerton, S. D. (2000). *A House Divided: Suspicions of Mother–Daughter incest.* New York, NY: Norton.

A riveting true story . . . meticulous and engaging.

—**Publisher's Weekly**

Abramson, P. R., & Pinkerton, S. D. (1995). *With Pleasure: Thoughts on the Nature of Human Sexuality.* **New York, NY: Oxford University Press.**

Stimulating, and informative, and written with ample wit.
> *— Scientific American*

A fresh and theoretically enticing approach to the study of human sexuality . . . Sure to spark intense debate.
> *— Kirkus Reviews*

Provocative.
> *— Seattle Times*

Abramson, P. R., & Pinkerton, S. D. (1995). (Eds.) *Sexual Nature/ Sexual Culture.* **Chicago, IL: University of Chicago Press.**

This volume contains much to stimulate, inform, and amuse, in varying proportions. What more can one ask?
> *— Journal of the History of Sexuality*

11

If we ever expect to solve the sexuality-based problems that modern societies face, we must encourage investigations of human sexual behavior. Moreover, those investigations should employ a broad range of disciplines — looking at sex from all angles, which is precisely what **Sexual Nature/ Sexual Culture** *does.*

 — American Scientist

Highly informative. . . .[T]here is none other quite like it.

 — Choice

It is useful to find this interesting question scientifically settled once and for all.

 — Times Literary Supplement

Illuminating.

 — Gay Times

Intriguing.

 — Feminist Collections

This book goes a long way towards bridging the gap between nature and nurture.

 — New Scientist

Abramson, P. R. (1984). *Sarah: A Sexual Biography*. Albany, NY: State University of New York Press.

How can so much intimate, destructive violence be part of our here and now, almost before our eyes? No novelist would dare, because fiction can neither resolve, nor even make reasonable, this material.

— *The Los Angeles Times*

A fascinating account . . . . A brief but memorable view of emotional survival.

— *Booklist*

DEDICATION

To my wife, Tania,

who made

Screwing Around

with Sex

fun

MANIFESTO

If happiness is equated with pleasure and if pleasure is fundamental to sex, then happiness and sex are inexorably linked. Governments therefore have a duty to respect the pleasures of their citizens, sexual freedom being one of them. Since the Constitution safeguards liberty and facilitates the pursuit of happiness, it's also the conduit for protecting sexual freedoms.

ACKNOWLEDGEMENTS

I started screwing around with sex in 1971. I was a 21-year-old graduate student at Connecticut College working on my master's degree. My professor, Bernard Murstein, began the semester by recommending that every student develop an independent research project. I was young and rebellious, and fascinated with psychoanalysis. Sex immediately came to mind.

My worry, however, was that every other student would come to the same conclusion, rendering the subject matter commonplace.

Thankfully, I was mistaken. Professor Murstein encouraged me to give sex a chance.

I started with masturbation. It's the way humans learn about pleasure and orgasm. The question, then, was how to go about studying it. Unlike most psychology departments, the one at Connecticut College did not require introductory psychology students to participate in psychological research. If you wanted volunteers, you needed to find them yourself.

I asked a friend of mine, a much better artist than I was, to draw posters advertising my study. Doubtful that anyone would show up for research on masturbation, she drew a nude heterosexual couple as an alternative. More than two hundred undergraduates wanted to participate.

I was throwing a party, or so it seemed, until my volunteers got to the questions about masturbation. Silence then crept over the room.

The study, which addressed how young people perceive the psychological consequences of masturbation, was eventually accepted for publication. The department chair, proud of my accomplishment, then asked me to give a lecture on this research. I didn't think anyone would be interested in a study on masturbation, but I agreed to the invitation nevertheless.

The study was incorrectly advertised; *soon-to-be-published research on sex,* it proclaimed. The room, not surprisingly, was packed once again. When I explained the misnomer in the announcement—that the talk was not about sex per se but instead about masturbation—all eyes drifted toward the exit.

I then decided that I should study sex guilt and transferred to the University of Connecticut. It was my ticket to a professorship at UCLA.

Over the course of a long career, I've had excellent mentors, colleagues, and students. I've also worked with superb litigators. Though I've written this book without reference to this illustrious assemblage, these collaborations have challenged, inspired, and sustained me throughout my 40-plus years at UCLA.

The late Philip Goldberg (Connecticut College) was the guiding light through my master's degree, and Donald Mosher (University of Connecticut) was the lodestar throughout my PhD. Both were spectacular. Julian Rotter (University of Connecticut) was instrumental to my development as well.

If Steve Pinkerton had been my only PhD student, that distinction alone would have been an enormous achievement. Steve is brilliant, hardworking, and a superb collaborator. We wrote countless articles and books together. Steve was everything a professor wants in a graduate student and so much more. Other PhD students of note include Monique Boudreaux, Paul Okami, Tracee Parker, and Stuart Perlman.

My forays into journalism have yielded delightful collaborations, too. Linda Williamson added edge to my writing, Leif Dautch broadened its social appeal, Vici Casana strengthened its clarity, and Drex Heikes gave it polish. My long-term bandmates Marc Bobro and Ian Putnam have been fantastic teammates as well.

I've also learned much from the litigators I've worked with and even more so from the cases we've worked on together. The repeat offenders include Richard Bennett, the late Rob Galler, Jack Girardi, Terry Gross, Tim Hale, John Howard, Bob Keese, Eugene Volokh, and Ron Zonen.

Wandering on this journey with terrific colleagues enlarged my horizons beyond measure. There is nothing described within this book that does not owe substantial gratitude to all of them.

The four reviewers of this book—Terri Conley, Keith Holyoak, Gregory A. Miller, and Catherine Ross—deserve my gratitude as well. I valued their comments emphatically.

Lastly, I want to extend my appreciation to the late Irving Maltzman and Gregory A. Miller. As fate would have it, they were the UCLA psychology department chairs who bookended my career. Irv, a colorful character, hired me, and Greg, a wise and noble colleague, capped it off.

This book, as the reader will soon discover, is rigorously academic but accessible to a fault. The format harkens back to the Enlightenment—David Hume and Thomas Paine come to mind—when learned authors published their work in the form of essays. My 21st-century spin on this approach is to focus on sex, from consent to sexual abuse to pornography and more, supplementing with case examples from an inadvertently wide-ranging career. The end result is short, sweet, and hopefully brainy enough to satisfy even the discerning scholar.

TABLE OF CONTENTS

CHAPTER 1

Indeed, Only Consent Is Consent

In the spring of 1975, while still a graduate student at the University of Connecticut, I gave a talk on data analysis and mainframe computers to the Psychology Department at Mansfield Training School (MTS). Mansfield was Connecticut's largest state institution for the developmentally disabled. The director of a federal grant on deinstitutionalization, Dr. Chris Birmingham, then asked me if I'd like a job. *Meet me at Psycho Patty's,* he said.

When I got there, a dive bar near the university, Dr. Birmingham wondered if I needed a drink.

Since this was ostensibly a job interview, I said, *No, I'm fine.*

A-ready 'ad a six-pack, Dr. Birmingham confided.

After a short conversation, I asked Dr. Birmingham why he was holding a harmonica. *Bought it today,* he said. *Thought I'd give 'er a try.*

Have you ever played one? I inquired.

No, he responded.

At which point Dr. Birmingham jumped on stage and started making odd noises with his newly acquired harmonica.

What da fuck?! yelled the drummer, a young woman with a Mohawk. A scuffle ensued, and a bouncer dragged Dr. Birmingham out the door.

Monday morning I received a telephone call from Dr. Birmingham telling me that I had gotten the job. When I asked him if there was anything I should read in preparation, he said I should study *Inside Linda Lovelace* and the *National Lampoon's 1964 High School Yearbook.*

Three weeks later Dr. Birmingham was gone. Suffering from bipolar disorder in an era when stigma was high and lithium was less widespread, Dr. Birmingham was fired after being arrested for jumping naked from a moving car in nearby downtown Willimantic, wearing only a sequined Moroccan slipper and a moose hat.

Despite my limited knowledge of developmental disabilities, MTS then made me the director of the federal grant. Being within shouting distance of a PhD was apparently good enough.

Deinstitutionalization

At that time state hospitals for the developmentally disabled, or for the mentally ill, for that matter, were largely custodial. Overcrowded and understaffed, such hospitals rarely offered treatment, and patients got worse. Sexual and physical abuse (by other patients and by staff) was common, too. Getting people out of institutions was thus the goal. Funding from Medicare and Supplemental Security Income (SSI) helped the transition by providing the necessary financial resources for placing people in community settings. Litigation was a big factor as well.

Kenneth Donaldson, allegedly paranoid schizophrenic, had been committed to Florida State Hospital. The facility had more than 5,000 patients, and effective treatment was nonexistent. Mr. Donaldson then petitioned the court, seeking to be released. The United States Supreme Court ultimately decided *O'Connor v. Donaldson* in 1975.

The hospital had defended itself by arguing that treatment wasn't critical because confinement alone was therapeutic. The Supreme Court disagreed, heralding a milestone for the deinstitutionalization movement. A state cannot constitutionally confine a person without treatment, it ruled, if that person is capable of living safely alone or with a responsible family member or friend.

What I discovered in 1975 at Mansfield was that deinstitutionalization focused almost exclusively on protections from harm. That should be a top priority, of course, but a person's other social needs were ignored. This situation was especially true of sex.

Sex and Developmentally Disabled Adults

Why should an institution care about sex? Can a developmentally disabled adult even consent to it? Pregnancy, abortion, contraception, homosexuality, and masturbation—a hornet's nest, Mansfield believed.

Parents of developmentally disabled adults were no less adamant. The very idea of sex was appalling. Unquestionably, the controversies that surround sex and the harm that manifests itself in the aftermath of unwanted sex reinforced this perspective.

Yet in a world narrowed by disability, consensual sex void of tangible harm could be a welcomed pleasure. This statement is not meant to minimize the grave risks of sexual assault to a vulnerable population. It is instead intended to acknowledge that sex has the potential to benefit all adults, developmentally disabled men and women included. If sex has value and if preventing sexual harm is essential, then developing age-appropriate sex educational protocols that are inclusive of everyone should be the foremost priority to insure that all participants are truly consenting to sex.

This imperative is by no means limited to developmentally disabled adults. When teenagers first start exploring sexuality, every step is critical, and consent is no less crucial. Sexually active college students are another case in point. Though young adults often move rapidly through the integrated steps of a sexual encounter, drug and alcohol abuse render decision making problematic. Was there really consent? Was it understood in the same way by both parties? Did someone misread cues? Was there sexual coercion? Though it's now facile in some circles to claim that affirmative consent is pointless, it's anything but that. Severe mental illness, for example, is another factor that compromises sexual negotiation and undermines the viability of consent.

At one extreme are situations like the Oregon case that I worked on as an expert witness; it involved an 18-year-old woman, Sharon Underwood, who had an IQ of 20 and was paralyzed on one side of her body. A male caretaker had raped her. Irrespective of her profound disabilities, Ms. Underwood was nonetheless the victim of dreadful sexual harm.

I worked on another expert witness case, this time in Rhode Island, that was more nuanced. Competence, credibility, desire, and harm were central questions therein.

The case involved a developmentally disabled woman in her late twenties, Debbie Clery, with an IQ of 65, who lived in a large community-based setting. Ms. Clery had accused a male caretaker, James Mervis, of sexual assault, only to retract the accusation one day later.

Ms. Clery initially said that Mr. Mervis had raped her while she was sleeping. Mr. Mervis denied it, and the facility believed him. When the police interviewed Ms. Clery, they, too, were skeptical of her accusation. Pressured and disheartened, Ms. Clery then recanted the accusation, after which, as punishment for lying, she was required to provide a written apology to Mr. Mervis.

Two months later Ms. Clery engaged in what was purported to be a brief consensual sexual act with Mr. Mervis. Repeated flattery and a phone call from his mother, of all things, convinced her to take a 45-minute bus ride, with one transfer, to Mr. Mervis's home. After watching pornography and engaging in anal sex, both of which confused her, she took the bus back to the community-based setting.

One month later Mr. Mervis was arrested for raping a nonambulatory, developmentally disabled woman in a disability van. The rape had been captured on a security camera. The police then tested the sheets that Ms. Clery had previously provided as evidence of her initial accusation. Mr. Mervis's semen was discovered there as well.

Is a developmentally disabled person competent enough to act with volition and then establish that he or she understands the nature and consequences of sex? What would it then take for third parties (e.g., administrations, police officers, and so on), if those criteria were met, to give credence to a sexual assault accusation?

Where Ms. Clery was concerned, the issues were intertwined. She was very curious about sex and had been taking birth control pills. She also had a part-time job, took special education classes at a local community college, and enjoyed circulating throughout her community, returning home at night to her board and care.

Presuming for a moment that Ms. Clery understood the nature and consequences of sex and that she knew how to make her sexual wishes apparent to others, the crucial question in her case was whether she was believable.

Consenting to sex is binary; it can be an affirmative yes or an affirmative no. It's bidirectional, too, since it requires mutual agreement. If a developmentally disabled adult, however, is perceived as unreliable, that adult is precluded from making effective use of consent. Sadly, Ms. Clery was dismissed as a liar, only to be later exonerated by evidence to the contrary.

Was Ms. Clery competent enough to give consent to sex? She understood that sex has risks—pregnancy and sexually transmitted diseases among them—and she was forthright about her desire to have a sexual relationship.

However, superficial appearances can also be deceptive; public personas can shield private vices. Though he dismissed Ms. Clery's accusations as preposterous, after he was arrested, it was discovered that Mr. Mervis had a long criminal record.

Did making a mistake, choosing to have sex with Mr. Mervis after the rape had occurred, pressured to do so no doubt, nevertheless serve as prima facie evidence that Ms. Clery could not give legal consent? Imprudent sexual choices are by no means the sole province of developmentally disabled adults; politicians readily confirm as much.

Affirmative Consent

The nuances of consent are fundamental to how all adults navigate sexual relations, regardless of age, gender, or mental status. These subtleties are also pivotal in how cultures define, prevent, and prosecute sexual assault. Yet, despite its significance, consent often relies only on implicit cues for rendition, such as interpreting a head nod, for example, observed by a partner and never documented in any form. If a disagreement later ensues, the contesting parties are reduced to arguing about the proverbial he said/she said when in fact nobody said anything.

Affirmative consent eliminates the guesswork of implicit cues. Only yes now means yes. It's sexual assault otherwise.

In many respects, affirmative consent and seat belts are similar. People initially hated wearing seat belts, but the mortality statistics for fatal car accidents ultimately held sway. Drivers are much more likely to survive a car crash if they aren't catapulted out of the car. Tangible harm was thus the leverage for making seat belt requirements persuasive.

Affirmative consent is advantageous because it takes some of the risk out of exploratory sexual encounters. Sexual assaults often happen when implicit sexual cues are misread—the touching of genitals, for example, being perceived as a green light to sexual intercourse. Affirmative consent is especially critical in teenage romances and other incipient relationships. Given the foreseeable psychic wounds that come from a sexual assault, affirmative consent reduces the incidence of harm.

The success of affirmative consent, however, relies

upon compliance. Teaching teenagers a carefully honed affirmative consent protocol before it's ever needed—for instance, in junior high school— and concrete training in the reporting of sexual assaults are essential in this regard. The same is true for developmentally disabled adults and other individuals who are compromised by intellectual and other psychological factors.

The bigger problem in sustaining a sexual relationship is not the aura of seduction, which some believe will be a casualty of an affirmative consent policy but instead is finding a way to make the joy last. Shared lust, time and time again, quickly dissolves into apathy.

The aim of getting prospective sexual partners to start talking rather than harming each other also serves the bigger goal of permanency. Talking about intimate matters can draw couples closer. Sharing values about the pacing of a sexual relationship is especially important as well since it prevents inadvertent harm and sends inappropriate suitors away. Perhaps such talk is unromantic in the traditional sense, but tradition isn't always virtuous for sex. Sexual harassment used to be a time-honored tradition in the worst sense of the word. It's still evident, in fact, in far too many contexts—in the food industry, for example.

Affirmative consent is also a vast improvement upon the haphazard negotiations in many incipient relationships, the onus of which is borne largely by young women. There need be no value judgments with affirmative consent. If a sexual act is void of tangible harm, the only requirement is verbal consent beforehand.

Not everyone, however, is a fan. Affirmative consent policy is just one more way of criminalizing sexual behavior, it has been said, and will increase the ever-expanding prison population. Affirmative consent also shifts the burden of proof from the accuser to the accused, whereby presumed innocence becomes instead the need to *prove* innocence.

The same could be said of marital rape. That designation criminalized another sexual behavior and increased the prison population as well. It shifted, in some respects, the burden of proof from the victim to the alleged raping spouse, but only after the crime itself gained widespread recognition.

The ubiquity of rape on college campuses is now having the same effect. It heralds the necessity of an affirmative consent policy that needs to be promoted at every opportunity as well as a behavioral requirement that must be expressed prior to the onset of any form of sex. Affirmative consent is also valuable to all sexually active populations because it eliminates the defenses of intoxication, the absence of overt resistance, and other excuses for nonconsensual sex.

Will women, claiming rape out of rejection, for example, abuse affirmative consent? False accusations are prevalent in all areas of sex crimes, and there is no reason to believe that affirmative consent is immune to misuse. That said, I do not believe it is or will be routinely misrepresented. Rape encompasses shame and stigma for women. It goes unreported largely for those reasons. To acknowledge a rape is extremely traumatic for a woman, and to have to testify in a criminal proceeding is even more so. Having the strength to step forward and accuse a rapist and being willing to testify against him are not efforts that can be easily minimized.

That college rapists don't fit an imagined rape profile, the sleazy ex-con or the habitual drug abuser, should surprise no one. Sex crimes are built on access to victims and obstacles to detection. The successful athlete, the good student, and the charismatic fraternity president raise fewer eyebrows. More likely than not, rapists are known to their victims.

Teenagers and Sexual Consent

Though the focus of affirmative consent has been largely on college campuses, a disturbingly high number of young people are victimized in high school and junior high school as well. According to one study by the Centers for Disease Control and Prevention, 42% of all female rape victims were first assaulted before they turned 18. Alarmingly, known assailants (friends, boyfriends, and extended family members) commit most sexual assaults, and perpetrators are likely to abuse multiple victims before they are caught.

The nuances of teenage sexuality are especially complex. For example, Cameron had ridden the bus to work everyday and met what he believed were two female college students, Nancy and Clarissa. Following six weeks of conversations while riding the bus together, Cameron invited both young women to a keg party at his apartment.

As the party was winding down at 3 a.m., Clarissa made it clear that she would enjoy having sex with him. Affirmative consent was evident prior to every sexual act. After hours of nonstop sexual adventures, Cameron and Clarissa fell asleep, only to be awakened at 8 a.m. by pounding on the front door. When Cameron heard the sound of the door falling off its hinges, he jumped out of a second-story window and ran away.

Clarissa, he later learned, was 13 years old. The man pounding at his door was her father. Cameron was arrested shortly thereafter for statutory rape.

The facts were disturbing: sex between a 20-year-old young man and a 13-year-old girl and an aftermath that could include a prison sentence and the man's lifetime registration as a sex offender.

Clarissa's videotaped confession was not particularly informative. She admitted to being at the party, smoking marijuana, and drinking beer, after which she had had sex with Cameron. Motives and other psychologically relevant information, however, were conspicuously missing.

The picture became clearer when I spent more time with Nancy and her parents. Both girls had apparently told each set of parents that they were sleeping at the other girl's house. Both girls had fully expected to spend the night at Cameron's party, each having brought backpacks with toothbrushes and a change of clothes. The girls had done everything possible, in manner and in dress, to pass as college students. Being able to spend the night away from home was simply another tactic to demonstrate that they were over 18 and living on their own. Though I never met Clarissa, I found that Nancy could easily pass for a college freshman.

Nancy also indicated that during the six weeks of their getting to know Cameron, the girls had never mentioned their ages or high school affiliations. Both were high school freshmen; Nancy was 14, and Clarissa was one week shy of that age.

Was it reasonable, in spite of her affirmative consent, to expect Cameron to conclude that Clarissa was a college student? She had come to a keg party without mentioning a curfew and carrying a backpack that included a change of clothing. She had smoked marijuana, had drunk beer, and had been motivated to engage in sex, details confirmed by both Cameron and Nancy. The sexual encounter was described as vigorous and enduring, behavior also believed to be consistent with that of a sexually active college student.

Affirmative consent obviously is not a remedy for all possible violations of informed consent. Clarissa's father's protests notwithstanding, the district attorney's office ultimately decided not to prosecute this case.

Age of consent can be very difficult to comprehend. Teenagers generally know that if a bank is robbed, convicted robbers go to jail. If a teenager has sex with another teenager, however, teens' comprehension of the legal consequences is less assured. A teenager might reasonably ask why it is a crime if the sex is voluntary and consensual. Or why it is a crime in one state but not in another. Even the definition of *sex* varies. A President of the United States once claimed that oral sex was not sex.

A teenager (18 or older) can also be convicted of statutory rape (i.e., sex between an adult and minor) without fully understanding what made his or her sexual conduct illegal. Though the general rule of thumb is that criminal liability rests upon a vicious will and an unlawful act, statutory rape is one of the exceptions. In statutory rape, the mental state of the defendant is irrelevant, purportedly to eliminate a specious defense that relies upon claims like *She looked 18* or *She said she was 18*.

But what if, instead, an 18-year-old is enjoying a sexual relationship with his 16-year-old boyfriend or girlfriend? Should we exclude a defense that relies upon a psychological explanation of the relationship itself? Unlike adults who prey upon minors, teenagers in romances incorporate sex for many reasons, including love. Might a high school student truly believe that he or she had a right to a consensual sexual relationship by virtue of the fact that relationships are sustained by psychologically and physically intimate exchanges?

Should the law prohibit a sexual relationship between an 18-year-old and a 16-year-old in all cases? Codes for the age of consent would confirm as much, but that rationale is usually framed around the implications of sexual intercourse—the sizable risks and responsibilities, for instance. But to high school students, sex is so much more than intercourse. What if a high school couple limited itself to mutual masturbation instead of having sexual intercourse? Is the age of consent still relevant? If not, why not—and what is the dividing line?

If romantic relationships in high school are inevitable, does such a relationship also imply tacit acceptance of sex—at least in some form—as a foreseeable outcome? One could argue that it's hypocritical to permit romance while criminalizing sex. Perhaps, instead, it's more reasonable to conclude that sex is an inevitable, or at least a common and foreseeable, consequence of romance and that schools thereby have a duty to provide sex education that reinforces both affirmative consent and safe sex alternatives.

There are undoubtedly many California high school students who also know that sexually intimate relationships between 16-year-olds and 18-year-olds are legal, for instance, in Connecticut but not in California. Those students might have good reason to believe that the laws should be equivalent across states, as the drinking age is. Perhaps they might also conclude that the Connecticut law provides a legal justification for an age-disparate high school sexual relationship in California as well.

Consider the age differences in the subplot of the 2011 movie *Crazy, Stupid, Love.* A 13-year-old boy (Robbie) is infatuated with a 17- year-old girl (Jessica) who happens to be infatuated with his middle-aged father (Cal). Various twists and turns transpire, but by the end of the movie, Jessica takes pity on Robbie and gives him a gift of nude photographs of herself to spark his masturbation. It's the warm and fuzzy finale of the PG-13 movie.

What are teenagers supposed to make of these age differences? Jessica is only 17, and the photographs were designed for sexual provocation. Is she distributing child pornography? What about sexually corrupting a minor? Robbie is only 13. In the movie, giving the nude photographs is an act of compassion, an older girl taking pity on the crush of a young boy.

Why, then, some kids may wonder, is it a crime in some jurisdictions for teenagers to exchange nude photographs on their iPhones in the real world? What role does consent play in *phonication* or *sexting,* for that matter? Do kids know that this conduct may be regarded as child pornography? It was innocent in *Crazy, Stupid Love*— empathetic, too.

Sex is a complex negotiation for an admittedly ephemeral act. Obtaining consent in a forthright and timely manner is a cumbersome hurdle—particularly for awkward teenagers, harder still if alcohol or other drugs are involved. Though most adults navigate these waters with success, the same may not be true for teenagers.

Then there is the issue of *informed consent* prior to the commencement of sexual activity. Adults not only need to show a willingness to participate in sex; they must also demonstrate that they understand the nature and consequences of their sexual actions. The same, obviously, must be required of teenagers; the risks of unwanted pregnancy and sexually transmitted infections would demand as much. The question, however, is how to insure *informed consent* with a sexually active teenage population? Saying yes is not synonymous with sexual literacy.

Under California law, legal consent to sex *presupposes an intelligence capable of understanding the act, its nature, and possible consequences.* Given the seriousness of this crime, it's curious that precise criteria, or even a test in a legal sense, are nonexistent. What does someone need to know to demonstrate comprehension? Should there be a written examination, like a driver's license test, that confirms one's sufficient knowledge (e.g., nature, consequences, affirmative consent, and so on) to legally consent to sex and documentation that would serve as evidence of such? It's certainly conceivable that a 16-year-old could have a better understanding of the nature and consequences of sex than a 19-year-old. Age, admittedly, is only a gross approximation of maturity. These issues are obviously even more complex for developmentally disabled adults.

Being old enough (however defined), being capable of acting voluntarily, affirming each step in a sexual encounter, and understanding the nature and consequences of sex are the four factors that transform sexual acts into legally permissible behaviors. Omitting any one of them turns sex into a crime.

Mental Illness and Sexual Consent

John Densmore was a 35-year-old schizophrenic man who had a sexual relationship with Father Wilson, a 42-year-old priest with AIDS. Consent was the fulcrum of a civil lawsuit investigating the nucleus of their sexual relationship.

After working in the aerospace industry, Mr.

Densmore had a severe psychotic break that required long-term psychiatric hospitalization. Following his discharge with a diagnosis of schizophrenia, Mr. Densmore put a premium on spiritual guidance. Stabilized through medication and psychotherapy, and supported by disability benefits from his former employer, Mr. Densmore then became a full-time volunteer at his church.

Soon thereafter Mr. Densmore saw a flyer advertising a lecture on prayer and meditation by the illustrious Bishop Beckett. Convinced that Bishop Beckett would be the perfect spiritual advisor, Mr. Densmore attended the lecture. When the lecture ended, Mr. Densmore ran to the podium and introduced himself, saying in effect that he was schizophrenic and had problems abusing drugs, too, but wanted to rectify his life through devotion to a spiritual advisor. Mr. Densmore then asked Bishop Beckett if he would assume that role.

Declining the offer, Bishop Beckett instead suggested that a better suited spiritual advisor was available, a colleague of his named Father Wilson, who happened to be at the lecture as well.

Though disappointed, Mr. Densmore nevertheless

agreed to meet Father Wilson. Mr. Densmore then confided to Father Wilson that he was schizophrenic and struggled with drug abuse. His marriage, he also noted, was falling apart as well.

Father Wilson assured Mr. Densmore that he would enjoy serving as his counselor, confidante, and spiritual advisor. The following week Father Wilson also began having sex with Mr. Densmore. Father Wilson was HIV positive at the time.

Deeply religious, psychologically impaired, and desperate for affection, Mr. Densmore quickly fell under Father Wilson's spell. Mr. Densmore left his wife and moved in with Father Wilson. Though the church vehemently condemned overt homosexuality, Father Wilson assured Mr. Densmore that God nonetheless approved of their sexual relationship.

One year into the relationship, Father Wilson was diagnosed with AIDS. The priest then convinced Mr. Densmore that he would nonetheless remain immune to HIV because a personalized prayer had been sent to a monastery that would guarantee it. Relieved, Mr. Densmore resumed having sex with Father Wilson.

Mr. Densmore eventually left Father Wilson in 2003 and moved to Iowa, spending time in psychiatric institutions there as well. Upon being discharged from his last hospitalization, Mr. Densmore began a one-year relationship with a woman. That relationship deteriorated into domestic violence, and Mr. Densmore was arrested and sentenced to prison.

Upon his release, Father Wilson pleaded with Mr. Densmore to return to their relationship. Homeless and mentally ill, Mr. Densmore went back to California to live with Father Wilson.

During yet another psychiatric hospitalization in 2007, Mr. Densmore told a psychiatrist, Dr. Chaudhary, about his sexual relationship with Father Wilson. Gravely alarmed, Dr. Chaudhary contacted a parish priest, Father Peters, and together they convinced Mr. Densmore to report his relationship with Father Wilson to church officials.

In November 2008, Mr. Densmore duly reported Father Wilson to church administrators. Consumed with guilt, Mr. Densmore then retracted his accusation, only to confirm it once again in April 2009.

Father Wilson conceded that he had in fact lived with Mr. Densmore intermittently for years, but he asserted that the relationship was chaste and thereby did not violate church policy. Shortly thereafter, however, Father Wilson acknowledged that a sexual relationship had existed as well. Father Wilson was defrocked, but the church allowed him to live in a church-affiliated monastery.

Strangely enough, the church official, Bishop Wellington, who had supervised the internal investigation of Father Wilson shortly thereafter disclosed his own gay sexual affairs, and he, too, was defrocked.

The church, as the defendant in civil litigation, nevertheless insisted that Mr. Densmore was an independent adult capable of giving consent to sex to Father Wilson and that he had done so repeatedly. The church also noted that Mr. Densmore had a history of sex with multiple partners. These sexual relationships, they believed, were prima facie evidence of his ability to give consent and of his intention to exercise his right to participate in sexual activity with more than one person. That Mr. Densmore left Father Wilson and then came back to him provided further proof, the church asserted, that Mr.

Densmore had acted with volition.

The church also emphasized that Mr. Densmore had provided informed consent to a medication clinical trial at a university hospital during the same time period. The church argued that if Mr. Densmore was capable of giving informed consent to receiving medication, then he was capable of providing informed consent to having sex as well.

The essential question underlying the civil lawsuit, however, was something else entirely. Was Mr. Densmore capable of understanding the nature and consequences of having sex with a priest with AIDS when fraud was also involved?

There's a difference between disingenuous revelations and outright fraud. Exaggerating one's wealth and accomplishments is also significantly different from lying about one's marital status, religion, or professional degree. While lying to seduce a fully functional adult is reprehensible, courts nevertheless recognize that insincerity is often an inevitable part of seduction. Lying to a severely mentally ill person is another matter entirely.

Consenting to sex does not constitute blanket

approval to having sex in perpetuity, either, or, for that matter, even to having sex the following day or night. People can change their minds. Was Mr. Densmore capable of realizing this notion?

Enticements are yet another story. Adults are presumed responsible for their sexual decisions, subtle pressures notwithstanding, if they act with volition and understand the nature and consequences of sex. When, however, do enticements—food, shelter, or drugs, for example— become coercion? Does the word of a priest carry disproportionate weight for a severely mentally ill person?

The church asserted that informed consent to sex was synonymous with other types of informed consent—to receiving medication or psychotherapy, for example. This particular belief was pivotal in this case as well.

Did Father Wilson intentionally defraud Mr. Densmore by purposely denying the risks of HIV? That matter alone would distinguish consent to sex from consent to participate in a clinical medication trial in which accurate information about the trial had been conveyed using several modalities, including talking with a physician, watching a video, reading a handout, and participating in a group discussion.

Mr. Densmore, fortunately, never contracted HIV, and after several years of negotiations, the civil litigation finally resolved in his favor.

Theft

Theft is the metaphor I use to explain the impact of sexual harm. If a car is stolen, the theft affects the owners in many ways. They feel vulnerable and angry and are frustrated by the inconveniences. They also fear that the theft could happen again. Perhaps next time the consequences would be worse, such as also involving a kidnapping, for example.

Yet it's easy to identify with these feelings because so many people own a car and depend upon its availability. A sexual theft, however, is that much more devastating and abiding. A sexual theft, née assault, is the plunder of something extraordinarily personal, extremely valuable, and especially well guarded. Our genitals are hidden, our nude bodies more generally are clothed, and our sexuality is shared with only a few people, all of our own choosing.

We reproduce and create families with sex, we build love with sex, and awe-inspiring pleasures are infused with sex. Sex is thus one of the most cherished aspects of human behavior.

When sex is stolen, through rape or sexual assault, it's a crippling and demoralizing loss. Cars are functional adornments, exchangeable and easily replaced. The theft of sex is mourned because it's critical to our self-identities. Our well-being, our sense of trust, and our place in the world are shattered in the aftermath of a sexual assault. How can we ever believe that the laws that govern human behavior will protect us in the future?

This metaphor came to me after I had worked as an expert witness on two separate civil litigation cases in which the victim had only learned of the sexual assault weeks after the fact. In the first case, a female coed in Wisconsin, Barbara, had been taking prescription medications that included side effects that were especially pronounced if the medicines were combined with alcohol. After a night of drinking moderately at a campus party with a group of friends, Barbara had passed out. Tom, a fellow classmate, volunteered to carry her back to her dorm room.

Something was odd when Barbara awoke the following morning. She wasn't wearing underwear. She didn't recall taking them off at night, but she didn't think that much about it until one week later when a girlfriend told her about a rumor she'd heard. Tom said that he'd had sex with Barbara.

During a subsequent criminal investigation, Tom confessed to the rape. Though Barbara had no memory of the assault, knowledge of it alone was crushing to her.

The second case, in Washington, DC, involved a 34-year-old married woman, Cynthia, who had gone to a concert with a group of old friends from college. They had hired a limousine so that they could drink without compromising their safety. Among the friends was a man, Oscar, who had had a brief affair with Cynthia four years before she had married.

Cynthia started feeling sick while riding in the limousine. Nauseous and unstable, she lowered the window and began vomiting. She passed out shortly thereafter. When the group got to the concert, everyone left the limousine except Oscar, who said that he wanted to make sure that Cynthia was ok. Oscar then rejoined the group 15 minutes later. Cynthia did not awaken until the following morning, six hours after she had been brought home after the end of the concert.

Like Barbara, Cynthia learned of the rape secondhand. This time, however, it had a twist. Oscar claimed that Cynthia had wanted to renew their affair and had consented to the sex. Cynthia, a married woman with a two-year-old child, was horrified and vehemently denied his account.

As part of the investigation of this alleged crime, the police interviewed the limousine driver. He confessed to having inadvertently lowered the window that separated the driver from the passenger side. Cynthia, he said, had looked like a rag doll while Oscar was raping her. She had been unconscious and unable to move her body parts.

Conclusion

Only when our culture fully appreciates the impact of sexual harm can we fully prevent its occurrence. Affirmative consent is but one piece of the puzzle, yet it's a critical piece, especially for the more vulnerable individuals in our midst—not only adults who are developmentally disabled or severely mentally ill, but also teenagers who need protecting, young adults in incipient sexual relationships, and others who have been compromised by drugs or alcohol. For the most part, these are women.

It is abundantly clear that men misread implicit sexual cues. If we continue to deny this fact, it's at our own peril. Men will also take sexual advantage of women incapable of resistance—being drunk, bedridden, whatever. Affirmative consent doesn't eliminate sexual assault; seat belts don't eliminate fatal car accidents, either. But affirmative consent helps establish more rigorous guidelines for sexual participation. Combined with the other criteria for consent—age, volition, and understanding the nature and consequences of sex—affirmative consent provides a more explicit template for successfully navigating a sexual encounter.

These issues are particularly important on a college campus because college students are sexually active but not necessarily psychologically sophisticated. Missteps are common, especially in interpersonal affairs, including sex.

Institutions—faith-based, university, military, social, and many others—prefer treating sexual assault as a violation of decorum that can be handled internally without the meddling influence of law enforcement. The euphemistic term *sexual misconduct* is a case in point.

Sexual misconduct is a demeaning and unnecessarily vague construct. It's not the worst idiom I've ever heard—*inappropriate relationship*, a phrase used by a female defense attorney representing a man in his 50s who had repeatedly raped a 12-year-old girl, taking the cake—but it's still poorly chosen nonetheless. Theft and robbery are not *property misconduct,* and homicide and aggravated assault are not *aggression misconduct.*

Rape and other sexual assaults are crimes. There is no reason to sanitize the language, except perhaps to add credence to a church's or university's decision to keep the jurisdiction within its boundaries.

Police departments have special investigatory teams for sex crimes because those investigations require special training. Law enforcement is so much better skilled at this undertaking, after which the relevant legal machinery, prosecutors and defense attorneys, can play its part as well. Though police involvement would eliminate an absorbing task now routinely assigned to university administrations, to do otherwise makes a mockery of a very serious crime that has profound psychological consequences for victims. Only consent is consent. Everything else is a sex crime and should be investigated and, when appropriate, prosecuted as such.

The picture of consent that emerges from this chapter is unavoidably dark—a bleak landscape populated by sex crimes and vulnerable populations. It need not be so, and that ultimately is the message intended. Sex has the capacity, by design, to be extraordinarily pleasurable. The regret and the fundamental injustice are that we as a culture have not done a better job of insuring that participants in sex are knowledgeable and safe. Comprehensive sex education, affirmative consent, and the swift prosecution of sex crimes are essential steps in correcting this inequity.

CHAPTER 2:

On the Precipice of Porn

On December 21, 1991, I received a telephone call from a postproduction executive at Knight-Time Entertainment. Her name was Nancy Brown. Dexter Knight, her boss, wanted to meet with me.

Knight-Time Entertainment was one of the nation's largest adult video companies. It delivered massive amounts of graphic action with trace elements of plot, generating millions of dollars per month.

I agreed to meet "Dex." A private plane took me to San Francisco and brought me back to Los Angeles the same evening. Mr. Knight's attorney, Leon Dreiser, joined us. Mr. Dreiser was a prominent First Amendment advocate with a history of defending pornography.

Dexter Knight was a towering man in his late 30s with spiky blond hair and a thick Cockney accent. He looked like an English gangster from the movie *Lock, Stock, and Two Smoking Barrels.* His vice president, Sugar Sid, was a portly man in his mid-50s with a Burberry raincoat nearly two sizes too small. The only evidence that he was cognizant was a whispered growl.

The third member of this troika, sitting in the preposterously long stretch limo, was Candy Barr. Ms. Barr, hailing from Asheville, North Carolina, was one of Mr. Knight's newest stars. Smiling and extending a hand toward me, beauty-pageant style with fingers pointed downward, she drawled, *Pro-fess-orrr.* Stills from her recent movies were then circulated while I sat transfixed watching mobsters and a porn star talking like effigies in books.

The last of our party, Mr. Dreiser, was retrieved from the Claremont Hotel. Following cursory introductions, he, too, asked to see the movie stills. *Wow, look at these,* he remarked, smiling to no one. After we arrived at Chez Panisse, Mr. Knight told his driver to take Ms. Barr to Union Square in San Francisco for a shopping spree. Mr. Dreiser then launched into an extended monologue about the third prong of *Miller v. California,* the Supreme Court case that defined *obscenity* (*whether the work, taken as a whole, lacks serious literary, artistic, political, or scientific* value).

What's the value of porn? he asked rhetorically. *People like it. It makes them happy,* he said. Then, lamenting the continued prosecution of X-rated films, he mused, *I'm now thinkin' that Dex should edit his whole damn catalog to reduce his vulnerability to an obscenity conviction.*

This, I learned, was where I came in. Mr. Dreiser wanted my opinion about which characteristics should be deleted from Knight-Time Entertainment videos that might offset their purported value. Serving as an expert witness in ensuing federal obscenity litigation was part of the arrangement, too.

The real question, then, was whether eliminating objectionable characteristics of pornography would diminish governmental sanctions. Dial-a-porn certainly had managed to gain FCC approval (as I learned in a previous case I had worked on for Pacific Bell), but that was largely framed as a freedom of speech issue within the context of a public utility. Devoid of that infrastructure, the question remained whether cultivating an incipient social conscience for pornography would protect it from obscenity indictments.

Standing on the curb after dinner, Mr. Knight asked his driver, *Where's Candy?*

I brought her to your house, boss, the driver replied.

Taking a deep breath, diamond shimmering in his front tooth, Mr. Knight screamed, *FOCK,* repeating it two more times. *Fock! FOCK!*

Now facing Mr. Dreiser and me, Mr. Knight moaned with regret, *I was going to 'ave 'er BLOW you guys.*

Bloody 'ell. She'd louvv it, mumbled Sid Sugar.

Damn, Mr. Dreiser griped instantly, ***I would have LOVED it, too!!***

No thanks, is all I said.

So much for my introduction to the world of pornography.

A movie about sex—adult consensual pornography, for example— is descriptive. It depicts a very frequent and naturally occurring event. If the event itself isn't illegal, why is its depiction potentially a crime?

Is it because sex is private, and when privacy is violated, a crime commences? If that were the case, a prenatal ultrasound might be criminalized. Perhaps it's the aggrieved viewer who makes pornography potentially obscene. *Miller v. California* asserts as much. Why, then, does this perception obscure the countervailing point of view that exists among pornographic aficionados?

We don't, for example, in other instances seek similar remedies for the unduly offended—people who object to another religion (or atheism) or oppose gay marriage, for example. At what point, then, do personal liberties offset official condemnation?

Watching pornography commonly appeals to male sexual fantasies. Though humans have the capacity to cognitively arouse themselves by thinking about sex, the task is much easier while watching a movie.

Why, then, Mr. Dreiser asked, *are women offended by it?*

Not all women loathe pornography, but men certainly enjoy it a great deal more. Perhaps it has something to do with masturbation. Men masturbate substantially more than women do.

It's also, no doubt, a function of our wiring. Men are more likely to be drawn to visual sexual cues than women are. Women, on the other hand, are responsive to a proxy for human contact, the vibrator. It, too, greatly enhances masturbation.

There's undoubtedly an economic issue operating here as well. X-rated pornography that appeals to heterosexual or gay men is cheap to produce, and the consumer market is large. X-rated pornography that appeals to heterosexual women, on the other hand, requires substantially more capital. It needs good acting, stories, locations, dialogue, relationships, intimacy, humor, and so on. A Hollywood-sized budget. The question then becomes, Is it worth the money and effort to discover the right formula for X-rated pornography for female viewers when the market for it is substantially smaller than the market for male pornography?

If a film can be made cheaply for half the population (men) who prefer that kind of stimuli, and who are much more likely to exhibit the behavior (masturbation) for which these films were designed in the first place, the pornography industry will target men over women. Though men and women are equally drawn to movies, some types of movies have greater appeal for one gender than for another.

All of that notwithstanding, the Justice Department still wanted to dismantle the adult pornography industry in the early 1990s by incarcerating the kingpins. If a business like Knight-Time Entertainment was a one-man show, it was potentially an effective strategy.

Mr. Knight was indicted for distributing a patently obscene movie in 1991. I was astonished, to say the least, to discover that by paying a two-million-dollar fine and wearing a monitoring device for six months thereafter, he quickly returned to business. The benefits of having a San Francisco penthouse, a famous chef, and a plethora of girlfriends surely stretched the concept of rehabilitation.

One year later the FBI arrested Mr. Knight again, now for distributing obscene materials in Greenville, South Carolina. This time, however, they were the newly edited Knight-Time Entertainment videos, per my suggestions, void of a long list of offending characteristics.

Mr. Knight, Mr. Dreiser, and I met again in San Francisco to discuss a defense strategy. I expected the unexpected, and I wasn't disappointed. The meeting itself was held in Mr. Knight's gym. His trainer was in attendance, too, a man who was nearly as wide as he was tall.

Before we began discussing the case itself, the conversation meandered to the best herbs for maintaining an erection. That, in turn, morphed into an even stranger monologue about Mr. Knight's trick for creating lactating breasts in pornography (a subgenre within a subgenre). The device itself was hokey; the actress simply held a tube under her breast, close to her nipple, and thereafter milk was squirted through the tube. Mr. Knight didn't stop laughing when telling the story: *Ya shoulda seen dem fockin milkers,* he said.

This, in turn, somehow reminded Mr. Knight of the time he created a two-foot-long papier-mâché penis for an actor to wear—and how wearing it went to the actor's head, so much so that the actor demanded a higher salary. *For a fockin' paper skin-flute,* Mr. Knight remarked.

Just as it appeared that Mr. Knight was finally winding down and about to discuss the impending criminal prosecution, he abruptly asked for a short recess. A Russian actress was waiting in his office.

Having now become accustomed to such delays, Mr. Dreiser and I retrieved other work and spent the intervening time productively. When Mr. Knight returned, without apology, 90 minutes later, we focused our attention on the Greenville litigation.

Mr. Dreiser presented a series of strategies designed to challenge the arrest. The search warrants, the specific offense (distributing obscene material), the grand jury process, and so forth were now all potentially subjects for dismissal. Mr. Dreiser then turned to me and asked, *What's our stance on the value of these videos*?

Having recently worked for the World Health Organization's Global Program on AIDS in Geneva, Switzerland, I reminded him of the connection that pornography had with safe-sex strategies. In an era (circa 1992) obsessed with sexually transmitted infections, it might be useful to emphasize that watching the edited videos has public health value as a safe-sex alternative. If such films were eliminated, a safe-sex option would be lost.

The counterargument is that pornography itself creates social harms. The videos being charged in Greenville, South Carolina, at the very least contained extensive cautionary preambles and had been edited to remove objectionable material. Every video seized in Greenville had also been sold legally during the same time frame throughout most of the United States.

I contacted organizations that were actively involved in AIDS prevention work, too. The Gay Men's Health Crisis (GMHC), for example, offered to provide evidence in support of my contention, but even more importantly, Dr. Jonathan Mann, former head of the World Health Organization's Global Program on AIDS (who later died, along with his wife, in the ill-fated Swissair Flight 111 crash), volunteered to testify in court. Both were planning to offer the opinion that masturbation to pornography was a healthy alternative to unprotected sex.

In order to convince a jury in Greenville that safe sex was essential for *their* state, I also gathered public health data on sexually transmitted infections in South Carolina. Without such data, jurors might conclude that masturbation and pornography were necessary evils in New York City but not in communities within the Deep South.

South Carolina had nearly 94,000 reported cases of gonorrhea in 1992. However, the true incidence of gonorrhea was probably larger because private physicians often fail to report cases from well-to-do patients. Even more startling was the incidence of gonorrhea in the *10- to*

14-year-old range: 1,550 cases. Early syphilis (11,546 cases) and HIV (3,130, cases)/AIDS (2,389 cases) reports were also substantial, suggesting that South Carolina needed safe sex just as much as the rest of the country did.

As I was preparing my charts, Mr. Dreiser interrupted me once again. *The Feds want to cut a deal,* I was told. The prosecution was asking for a $500,000 fine. It would cost Mr. Knight at least half that to defend himself, with no guarantee of winning. The money would also be used for a rape crisis treatment center, a solution that was acceptable to Mr. Knight as well.

During the next six months, pornography went through the roof. The prices of video players were substantially cheaper than they had been, and Knight-Time's sales expanded dramatically.

Then, once again, Mr. Knight was arrested on April 23, 1993. Sixteen Knight-Time Entertainment videos had been confiscated in Cummings, Georgia.

The FBI had also raided the Knight-Time Entertainment corporate offices in San Francisco. The United States District Court of Northern California had issued a search warrant that demanded a photograph of Mr.

Knight, photographs of his office building, all of his business records, and every interracial and all-black video in his warehouse.

Confiscating black and interracial pornography for a trial in Georgia was the Justice Department's tactic for inflaming racial prejudice among Southern jurors. If I hadn't seen the search warrant myself, I would never have believed it.

Mr. Dreiser filed a civil rights claim arguing that the federal government was using racial prejudice as a prosecution tactic. He won the motion, and every video that had been confiscated in the San Francisco warehouse was dropped from the case. The venue was changed as well, moving slightly southwest from Cummings to Atlanta, Georgia.

What remained in this case, now titled *United States of America v. Dexter Knight*, were the 16 videos that had been confiscated in Cummings. One, in particular, is worth noting. Twelve minutes long, it was a gay male film titled *Let My People Go Wild with My Ass.* It starred three male actors, two of whom were white and one African American. The film ended with a double anal penetration.

Once more I delved into the relevant statistics on sexually transmitted infections (STI), this time for Georgia. The Centers for Disease Control (CDC), also located in Atlanta, provided epidemiologists capable of testifying about gay male pornography and safe sex.

Knight-Time Entertainment had sold more than 40,000 adult videos in Georgia during the previous year. Catalog purchases totaled more than 70,000 copies, a figure that did not include sales from adult video stores or adult video rentals. These data were to be used to demonstrate that Georgia tolerated adult consensual pornography in its communities.

A jury would then be asked to decide whether the United States had proved beyond a reasonable doubt that Mr. Knight was the chief executive officer of Knight-Time Entertainment; that Knight-Time had sent the 15 confiscated videos to Cummings, Georgia; and that the videos themselves were in fact obscene according to *Miller v. California.*

At trial, *Let My People Go Wild with My Ass* was broadcast at full volume on a large screen in a United States Federal Courtroom. Though extremely sexually explicit, it also contained numerous preamble warnings and had been edited, for example, to remove disparaging language. The film began and ended with commentary about sexual rights and the Constitution.

These facts were significant because *Miller v. California* uses the phrase *taken as a whole* when describing obscene material. If the movie, for instance, had funny parts or a thought-provoking preamble, a juror could conclude that the *whole* movie was not obscene.

The big question, however, was whether it had *value. Let My People Go Wild with My Ass* was devoid of plot, the prosecution noted, and the dialogue was insipid. Plots and dialogue, the prosecution asserted, are the bedrock of value and of First Amendment protection, for speech in particular.

On cross-examination by the prosecution, I had the opportunity to argue otherwise. Speech, I reminded the jury, is protected because it conveys *ideas.* Films are protected speech because they, too, convey ideas. A silent film can convey an important idea no less than a foreign language film, in which the dialogue is incomprehensible. A photograph can convey an idea as well.

Thirty minutes later I received another call from Mr. Dreiser. *Pack it up. We're outta here.*

The Justice Department had just offered yet another deal. When I reminded Mr. Dreiser that he was done dealing, he paused and then said, *Dex didn't want to go to prison. Me or you, we'd do the time, play pinochle for six months, and then walk out.*

I remember thinking, *I wouldn't want to go to prison, either,* and I've never played pinochle in my life.

Awaiting a flight out of Atlanta, Mr. Dreiser predicted that if Bill Clinton got elected in 1992, *the Feds would get out of porn.* As it turned out, he was right once again.

Stanley v. Georgia

I cut my teeth on pornography in 1973. My PhD advisor at the University of Connecticut, Dr. Donald Mosher, had been a member of the 1969 President's Commission on Obscenity and Pornography. Our collaborations had begun in the aftermath of those proceedings.

The story begins with Robert Eli Stanley. Mr. Stanley was the infamous appellant in the Supreme Court case of *Stanley v. Georgia* (1969).

It started with a search warrant. The police (state and federal) entered Mr. Stanley's apartment in the hope of finding incriminating evidence of illegal gambling. What they found instead was something more provocative. While rummaging through a desk drawer in Mr. Stanley's upstairs bedroom, the police discovered three reels of 8-millimeter film, one with the tantalizing title *Young Blood.*

When the unsuspecting Mr. Stanley returned home, he was arrested and subsequently indicted, tried, and convicted (on January 19, 1967) for knowingly possessing obscene material in violation of Georgia law. Mr. Stanley's defense was that the films weren't his. A guest at a Labor Day party had left them in his apartment. Mr. Stanley then had thrown them in a desk drawer and had never watched them.

Mr. Stanley's protests notwithstanding, a Georgia trial court concluded that the films were his because he possessed them and that they had been viewed in his home, a film projector in the apartment serving as the proverbial smoking gun. The judge also noted that the frayed appearance of the films suggested that they had been repeatedly viewed. Though there was no evidence that Mr. Stanley had distributed the movies, the trial court also concluded that an obscenity conviction was not dependent upon distribution.

Wesley Asinof, Mr. Stanley's appellate attorney, appealed the case to the Georgia Supreme Court. On April 9, 1968, the Georgia Supreme Court upheld the findings of the lower court. Mr. Stanley then appealed his case to the United States Supreme Court.

Stanley v. Georgia was argued on January 14 and 15, 1969.

Mr. Asinof affirmed that every Supreme Court obscenity decision prior to 1969 had been designed to punish the *distribution* of obscene materials. These rulings, he noted, were a reasonable use of governmental power to regulate public actions. However, none of these decisions, he emphasized, were designed to punish the mere possession of obscenity, thereby making Mr. Stanley's arrest and conviction unconstitutional.

More importantly, Mr. Asinof emphasized that Mr. Stanley's arrest depended in large part upon the assumption that Mr. Stanley knew that the films were not merely pornographic but were *obscene* and thereby illegal. The Supreme Court itself, Mr. Asinof avowed, had great difficulty defining *obscenity*. How could any American citizen make this determination any more easily than the United States Supreme Court? Mr. Asinof urged the justices to hold that obscene (or potentially obscene) materials could not be criminalized when possessed in the privacy of one's own home.

Suppose, Mr. Asinof hypothesized, that someone distractedly doodles an explicitly sexual drawing of a couple engaged in oral genital sex. When finished, this person puts the doodle in a drawer. The next evening, a police officer enters the house on some other pretext, looks in the drawer, and discovers the drawing. The police officer is offended by the drawing, concludes that it's obscene, and arrests the artist.

Are we, Mr. Asinof then asked, supposed to arrest doodling American citizens for the private possession of an image that may or may not be obscene?

The State of Georgia disagreed. *If obscenity*, Assistant District Attorney J. Robert Sparks argued, *is a crime, it should remain criminal whether distributed or possessed.*

The Supreme Court announced its decision on April 7, 1969. Limiting itself to the question of whether the State of Georgia had violated Mr. Stanley's First Amendment rights by punishing him solely for the private possession of obscene material within his home, the court overturned Mr. Stanley's conviction.

Their reasoning went as follows: First, all prior obscenity cases that the Supreme Court had ruled on had been concerned with the *distribution* of obscene materials. The Court explained that a stricter standard is used for distribution because such materials may offend an unwitting recipient or fall into the hands of children. Mr. Stanley, who was a bachelor and lived alone, clearly possessed this material solely within his own home, making the facts of this case different from those of its predecessors.

Second, the Supreme Court reiterated that the First Amendment recognizes and rigorously protects the right to receive information and ideas *regardless of their social worth.* Though exceptions to this blanket approval have been recognized since *Stanley* was decided (child pornography being a prime example, in large part because it depicts a felony crime against a child and encourages a market for the perpetuation of such crimes), the Supreme Court in *Stanley v. Georgia* asserted that despite whatever justifications existed for regulating obscenity, such justifications did not reach into the privacy of one's own home. The Court concluded, *If the First Amendment means anything, it means that a State has no business telling a man, sitting alone in his own home, what books he may read or what films he may watch. Our whole constitutional heritage rebels at the thought of giving government the power to control men's minds.*

The President's Commission on Obscenity and Pornography

The fallout from *Stanley v. Georgia* was immediate. Congress authorized two million dollars to fund a presidential commission to study pornography in the United States. The ostensible purpose of the commission was to create a powerful tool for eradicating pornography for once and for all.

A blue-ribbon panel of professors was appointed to the commission, drawn primarily from social science departments at prominent universities throughout the United States. One was Dr. Donald Mosher, my future PhD advisor.

Each expert was provided with a uniform set of six pornographic films made by the Institute for Sex Research in Hamburg, Germany. The films had been designed and distributed solely for research purposes. They depicted either heterosexual sex or masturbation. The same actor and actress were used in each film, and the content was controlled and systematically varied. There were, for example, a *Petting One* film and *Petting Two* film, with the latter depicting more sexual content short of intercourse. There were also an *Intercourse One* film and *Intercourse Two* film, with the latter, once again, showing more variety in the sexual content. The final two films consisted of a male masturbating to orgasm and a female masturbating to orgasm. Both masturbation films followed the exact same sequence and timing.

The *Final Report of the President's Commission on Obscenity and Pornography* was due on September 30, 1970. However, a preliminary draft of the report had been leaked to a House of Representatives subcommittee prior to its publication. The draft report emphasized that the consequences of viewing pornography were benign, and it reaffirmed the findings in *Stanley v. Georgia.*

Congress fumed. This was hardly the sought-after antipornography ammunition it had hoped for. When the commission's report was finally published, Vice President Agnew proclaimed, *As long as Richard Nixon is President, Main Street is not going to turn into smut alley.* President Nixon commented as well, asserting, *So long as I am in the White House, there will be no relaxation of the national effort to control and eliminate smut from our national life.*

Charles Keating, an antipornography activist who had been an advisor to the presidential commission, was equally chagrined. In a separate dissenting report, Mr. Keating accused the commission of being *dedicated to a position of complete moral anarchy.*

It's ironic, certainly in hindsight, that these three individuals—Mr. Agnew, Mr. Nixon, and Mr. Keating—all fell far from grace. Vice President Agnew was forced to resign in 1973 over illegal kickback payments, President Nixon was forced to resign the presidency in 1974 over the Watergate burglary and cover-up, and Mr. Keating received a 12 ½-year sentence for securities fraud, conspiracy, and racketeering after the collapse of Lincoln Savings and Loan in the early 1990s.

After all the hoopla had died down, the commission's report itself collected dust in university libraries throughout the United States. If indeed it drew any attention on a college campus in 1970, it was competing with the more electrifying issue of the Vietnam War. The vicissitudes of pornography failed to capture the intellectual attention of the academic world—except, curiously, mine.

Miller v. California

Studying pornography is at best a dubious expertise, or so one would think. What benefit could possibly accrue from an academic knowledge of pornography?

Two months after arriving at UCLA as an assistant professor of psychology in 1976, I was asked by Stanley

Fleishman, a prominent First Amendment advocate, to serve as an expert witness in an obscenity trial. Fleishman had represented, among others, the novelist Henry Miller and had previously argued before the United States Supreme Court. Fleishman was now defending a movie that the State of California deemed obscene. He asked me to watch the movie and offer my opinion of it.

In 1970, Marvin Miller (no relation to Henry) was a bookseller with a big idea. He wanted to sell books about sex, but he also realized that people were too embarrassed to buy them in a bookstore. Mr. Miller then decided to create a mass-mailing brochure advertising four books: *Intercourse, Man-Woman, Sex Orgies Illustrated,* and *An Illustrated History of Pornography.* A small sample of the books' pictures and drawings were shown in the brochure.

Five of Mr. Miller's brochures had been sent in an unmarked envelope to a restaurant in Newport Beach, California. When the manager's mother opened the envelope and saw the pictures from *Sex Orgies Illustrated,* she called the police. Marvin Miller was arrested and convicted of *knowingly distributing obscene matter* in violation of California Penal Code §311.2 (a).

Like Mr. Stanley before him, Mr. Miller appealed his conviction all the way to the United States Supreme Court, hence the 1973 case *Miller v. California,* which established the current definition of *obscenity.* Unlike Mr. Stanley's, however, Marvin Miller's conviction was upheld.

Miller's attorney, Burton Marks, made two basic arguments: First, the definition of *obscenity* is vague and inoperable. Marvin Miller was thus being convicted of obscenity even though he was incapable of determining it on his own. If a governmental review board, for example, had told Mr. Miller that his brochure was obscene, and he had distributed it anyway, Mr. Marks asserted, that situation would make for a reasonable criminal conviction.

A definition of *obscenity,* Mr. Marks also declared, must be based upon a national standard. Just because someone in Montgomery, Alabama, or Newport Beach, California, was offended by a picture or drawing, this situation should not be the basis for determining whether something is truly obscene and void of constitutional protection. If the Constitution represents federal law, then questions about constitutional protection should be based on national standards.

Michael Capizzi, an assistant district attorney from Orange County, California, argued otherwise. He asserted that whatever standard was used—city, state, or national—Marvin Miller's brochures were obscene in each and every case. Furthermore, if the Supreme Court were to adopt a national standard, it would punish liberal and conservative communities alike. Liberal communities might want access to films that the national standard deemed obscene, whereas conservative communities would have to tolerate material that its constituents found offensive.

The Supreme Court was divided in its opinions, ruling in a 5–4 split that Marvin Miller's conviction should be upheld. Chief Justice Burger, writing for the majority, emphasized three factors: The brochures were hard core; they had been sent to unwilling recipients; and local communities, the Court concluded, could set their own standards for obscenity.

Justice William Douglas disagreed: *To give the power to the censor, as we do today, is to make a sharp and radical break with the traditions of a free society.* Justice Douglas's protest notwithstanding, *Miller v. California* became the new law of the land.

Sitting in Mr. Fleishman's conference room in the fall of 1976, I faced the same task—to watch the movie. What I was watching was a Caucasian male having sexual intercourse with an African American female. The film looked no different than the Commission on Pornography *Intercourse One* film. The male looked muscular, the female looked voluptuous, and they were having sexual intercourse in the same position throughout the film—side-to-side, or "spooning," with their backs to the camera.

As the film was ending, however, the actress rolled over, and she had a penis. The couple had been having anal sex, but this fact was never apparent to the viewer. A transgendered person in heterosexual pornography was unusual for the era, hence the prosecution.

It's a curious film, I said, *but the sexual content is no more explicit than* [that in] *the films distributed for research purposes. If anything, it accurately depicts the identity of a transgendered person. That portrayal alone, one could argue, is its value.*

Though this film was not successfully prosecuted, it raised other issues for me. What if our moral precepts are so entrenched that they are immune to alteration except when justly challenged? What, then, would constitute such a challenge? How persuasive, compelling, or jolting would the challenge have to be? Would pornography containing a transgendered actress fit the bill?

There are, admittedly, many horrifying atrocities that are profoundly shocking, the savage nature of which overwhelms the senses. Viewing nonviolent adult consensual pornography, however, is not one of them. The real question, then, is whether harm born out of disgust negates protecting shocking ideas that are otherwise defensible on free-speech grounds.

Attorney General Edwin Meese's Commission on Pornography

In 1983, I was drawn back into the study of pornography. I was a visiting professor of psychology at Kyoto University in Japan. Vending machines for pornography there had caught my interest, the violent sexual imagery in particular, in which the genitals, curiously, were never depicted—a nude woman gagged and bound by ropes while receiving an enema being a case in point.

Yet Japan had one of the lowest sex-crime rates of any industrialized country in the world. American social scientists would have predicted otherwise.

Japan tolerates violent imagery because it believes that emotions released in fantasy will diminish their presence in the real world. Perhaps that's true in a country like Japan where impulse control is valued, and the family is revered.

That idea, paradoxically, catapulted me into yet another national debate about pornography when I was invited to become a member of Attorney General Edwin Meese's Commission on Pornography. The Meese Commission, like its predecessor, was designed to eradicate a pestilence.

The Meese Commission did not fund original research. It based its conclusions solely upon testimony provided to the commission itself. The advantage of this strategy was two-fold. It hedged its bets by eliminating the funding of research in which the outcome was uncertain, and it could selectively favor testimony in its final report.

The Meese Commission was designed to capitalize upon feminist writings, that of Andrea Dworkin in particular, that had equated pornography with violence toward women. It thereby fashioned itself as a compassionate governmental watchdog protecting women from harm.

Speaking to college students at the University of Massachusetts in 1977, Ms. Dworkin had asserted: *Pornography is the propaganda of sexual fascism . . .* [and] *sexual terrorism.* Carrying this theme forward in 1981, Ms. Dworkin wrote in *The Los Angeles Times* that *pornography is dangerous and effective* [because it] *incites violence against easy targets — women and children.*

The Meese Commission did not, however, limit itself to the inclusion of only the Andrea Dworkins of the world. Both sides of the political spectrum, ranging from former porn stars to victims of sexual assault, were invited to provide testimony as well. So, too, were a group of dissenting social scientists, including me.

My work in Japan was tailor-made for testimony before the commission, particularly in the debate about violence and pornography. It was also a counterpoint to the claims of Ms. Dworkin. Perhaps not surprisingly, when the *Final Report of Attorney General Edwin Meese's Commission on Pornography* was published in July 1986, none of my testimony was mentioned. The only acknowledgement of my presence as a speaker before the commission is that I am listed as the last witness to testify in Houston, Texas.

Despite the momentum of the antipornography movement, the Meese Commission ultimately fell upon its own sword, rendered impotent by a self-inflicted pornographic wound. The commission inexplicably decided to include pornography within the *Final Report* itself, an excerpt from the pornographic novel *Tying Up Rebecca*. For example: *As Schultz watches, masturbating himself, Becky urinates into the toilet. Some of the urine splashes and extinguishes Mr. Schultz's pipe. He ejaculates on his clothes[,] and Patty enters the bathroom dressed only in panties and bra.*

Consensual nonviolent pornography is sexual imagery that excites some people (primarily men) and offends others. Feckless humans, however, commit crimes in its name. To argue, as some have, that the message of pornography is rape is specious at best.

The First Amendment

Why does pornography have First Amendment protection? Women, for example, are routinely slashed in teenage horror films or thrive on mutilation in others (e.g., *The Lobster*). Why do we applaud dubious plot lines as long as the production values are high?

The First Amendment, as noted previously, protects all ideas—not simply florid or articulate ones. The freedom of speech is extended to all speakers, those who can wax prosaic and those who cannot.

What is the protected *idea* in pornography?

Pornography is a provocative vehicle for depicting the idea that sex is pleasurable. The message is valuable because it serves as a counterweight to the Bible or other religious texts that reserve sex for reproduction. Ideological diversity is essential to the freedom of speech.

If nonviolent adult consensual pornography is largely the embodiment of the idea that sex is fun, why then is it so threatening? The idea itself, it would seem, is hardly a menace to social order.

It is threatening, I believe, because it challenges conventional morality in a particularly provocative manner: it conveys the notions that monogamy and reproduction are irrelevant, that courtship is a waste of time and money, and that guilt about sex is absurd. In the great marketplace of ideas, pornography is, as David Richards has artfully observed, a *unique medium of a vision of sexuality[,] . . . a view of sensual delight in the erotic celebration of the body, a concept of easy freedom without consequences, a fantasy of timelessly repetitive indulgence.*

Child Pornography

Tod Impara was a correctional officer at Pelican Bay Maximum Security Prison in Crescent City, California, where inmates spend up to 23 hours of every day in a 10 x 20-foot concrete cell. Mr. Impara was also one of the most notorious child pornographers in the United States. I served as a consultant in his criminal prosecution and served as an expert witness in the civil lawsuit that followed.

Computer savvy, Mr. Impara had a plan. Together with his friend Jack Sobell, he would create a website that would broadcast adult–child sex in real time. Viewers could then transmit directorial comments, and the adult participants, Mr. Impara and Mr. Sobell, could alter the sexual acts.

Though they had a global database of pedophiles, there was still the issue of finding children to participate. Mr. Impara, who had two young daughters, decided to target his daughter's friends, each of whom, ironically, also had a parent who was a correctional officer at Pelican Bay. Eventually, Mr. Impara coerced one 12-year-old, Pamela, into participating in sexual acts, ultimately culminating in intercourse.

Seven months later, the FBI discovered the site, Newfolklore. Three months earlier Mr. Impara's site had operated openly as Sexykids4u. When the FBI raided Mr. Impara's home, they caught Mr. Sobell having sex with Pamela while Mr. Impara was filming the act. Interpol simultaneously raided the homes of every person who had logged onto the site as well, apprehending pedophiles from Australia to Finland.

Pamela testified at the criminal hearing on the promise of anonymity. To insure as much, the court issued an order prohibiting any depiction of Pamela or her family. When the verdict was read, a 200- year prison sentence for both perpetrators, one television station ignored the court order so it could capture the reaction of Pamela's parents. *What a relief,* the television commentator said, as her parents' faces appeared on camera. This news coverage was also broadcast to inmates at Pelican Bay, immediately making Pamela's father, and by extension, Pamela herself, identifiable.

The TV station, owned by a large media conglomerate, claimed it had a First Amendment right to film and broadcast critical news, particularly a case of this nature. The attorney Terry Gross successfully argued otherwise, resolving the first aspect of the civil lawsuit initiated by Pamela's family.

Her family, not surprisingly, also sued the Impara and Sobell estates, the former of which was quite sizable since Mr. Impara had inherited a substantial amount of beachfront property in the Crescent City area. The late Robert Galler represented the plaintiffs. He successfully resolved his portion of the civil lawsuit as well.

How does a father of two daughters, a correctional officer, no less, mastermind a multinational crime of this nature? Mr. Impara did very little to disguise the web-based infrastructure. He instead put his efforts into grooming the victim, using attention and flattery to minimize disclosure. Disclosure apparently was Mr. Impara's only concern.

Though Pamela had been puzzled by the intense focus on her attractiveness, it came at the cost of her ever-present panic and dread. How could she ever escape the self-loathing? Who would recognize her? She was profoundly depressed and hypervigilant to cues of the abuse, typical symptoms of victims with posttraumatic stress disorder.

Child pornography is prima facie evidence of a crime against a child. Sexual acts involving minors, particularly acts between an adult and a prepubertal child, are also easy to identify and prosecute. Criminalizing the *possession* of child pornography, as a further disincentive aimed at reducing the commercial market for child pornography, decreases the sexual exploitation of children. Punishing both sellers and buyers is thus an effective strategy for minimizing the frequency of this crime.

Newton v. Allen

I've served as an expert witness in many other child pornography cases. I'm including one more because it contained a documentary record, in the form of more than 3,000 named and dated pornographic slides, of 24 preschool-age children. This case was especially important to me for many reasons, most notably because it further strengthened my understanding of the impact of child sexual abuse.

In 1979, I started writing a book about a former student of mine titled *Sarah: A Sexual Biography.* It was about the impact of child sexual abuse. Publicity surrounding the book, published in 1984, drew me into the case (*Newton v. Allen*) to be discussed herein.

Though Sarah's story is depressingly familiar today, inhabiting everything from soap operas to major motion pictures, this was not the case in the late 1970s. The vast nature and unremitting impact of child sexual abuse were still deeply undercover. When Art Siedenbaum, the book review editor at *The Los Angeles Times*, reviewed my book, he asked: *How can so much intimate, destructive violence be part of our here and now, almost before our eyes? No novelist would dare, because fiction can neither resolve, nor even make reasonable this material.*

Leslie Ellis, another former student of mine who was working as a clerk for the attorneys Jack Girardi and Robert Keese at the time, read the Seidenbaum review. Her employers had recently begun representing the aforementioned 24 plaintiffs from the preschool child pornography case. I worked for nearly five years as an expert witness in *Newton v. Allen*, most of my time spent with the victims and their families.

Alicia Allen ran a very well-known and highly respected preschool in Riverside, California. The mayor had made a much-publicized visit there, and a photographic record of his appearance adorned the walls.

Alicia's husband, Dr. Peter Allen, was a physicist by training and an amateur photographer as well. The couple had met at a photography exhibit at the University of California–Riverside. Dr. Allen was 27 years older than his wife.

Though the preschool was locally renowned, it was not without its problems. Twice in 1979 the police received complaints that Dr. Allen had sexually molested a child.

However, those investigations and subsequent surveillance had been inconclusive.

This all changed in October 1980 when 5-year-old Melissa Newton told her parents that Dr. Allen had taken *nekid pictures of me. He touched my privates[,] too.*

The Newtons immediately confronted Ms. Allen. She had no idea what they were talking about, she said, but she assured the Newtons that she would investigate.

The next day Dr. Allen reached into his briefcase and retrieved an 8 x 10 photograph. He handed it to Mr. Newton. *I have no idea what Melissa was talking about*, Dr. Allen said. *She was wearing this beautiful red dress yesterday, so I took a picture of her in it.*

That night the Newtons confronted their daughter again. Yes, she said, Dr. Allen had taken a picture of her in the red dress. Later that day, however, he had taken her to his home, where nude photographs had been taken while she sat on his dresser. The details of Melissa's disclosure convinced her parents to go directly to the police.

Armed with a search warrant, the Riverside Police Department raided the Allen home on November 5, 1980. In the closet of Dr. Allen's bedroom (his wife had a separate bedroom), they found more than 3,000 pornographic slides of children between 2and 5 years of age. Each slide was labeled and dated in Dr. Allen's handwriting; his hand was evident on the slides as well. Twenty-four different children were depicted, with dates on the slides ranging from 1974 to 1980.

The female genitals, held open by Dr. Allen's hand, were evident in the majority of slides. Other slides contained images of the anus, penis, scrotum, and buttocks.

Dr. Allen was booked immediately. A preliminary hearing began shortly thereafter. Many parents and one child provided testimony. Especially tragic was the discovery that many children had disclosed to their parents that they were being sexually molested *prior* to the raid of the Allen home. These parents, now beside themselves, tearfully recounted how they had dismissed the claims as incredulous without ever notifying the police.

At the criminal trial, many of the same parents testified again for the prosecution. Two detectives and a handwriting expert from the Riverside Police Department testified as well. Two clinical psychologists and a psychiatrist who evaluated Dr. Allen were the final members of the prosecution team.

Dr. Allen's father testified for the defense, as did two of his former high school teachers, his high school principal, and a high school friend. Two psychiatrists and a clinical psychologist who had seen the child pornography also spoke on his behalf as well.

I did nothing wrong, asserted Dr. Allen in the criminal proceedings. *I took these pictures because I am doing longitudinal research on child development.*

If this is true, asked the district attorney, *where is the evidence that you were working on a scientific study or writing a scientific report?*

I've been swamped, Dr. Allen replied. *I've been so busy I haven't had the time to put it together yet.*

Who was this "study" supposed to benefit? the district attorney then inquired.

I believe, Dr. Allen responded, *the children were happier at preschool than at home, and if they are having problems now, it's their parents' fault. Their parents have no education; they are stupid. I did a marvelous job at the preschool for the community and offered a beautiful service that has been destroyed. I don't think I want to help these people anymore. They have been so hateful. If we do open another preschool, it will be far, far away, preferably in another state. You know the State's attitude toward nursery schools[,] and the State certainly isn't protecting me.*

Do you think, the district attorney asked, *that these parents want your help anymore?*

I'm in a better position, Dr. Allen replied, *to judge what is good for the child. The parents are doing bad things that deprive the child of experience that a child ought to have, which only I can supply.*

You took pornographic slides of these children, the district attorney continued. *Didn't you think that this posed a risk to these kids?*

Since there was nothing wrong with what I did, Dr. Allen proclaimed, *I didn't see any risk. I couldn't have predicted what happened. I like children. I like photography. It was really a good time thing. Maybe it's not normal, but it's all right. Children are nice and beautiful. It may be abnormal because we say it is, basically, but it's not wrong.*

These are pictures, the district attorney continued, *that contain your hands on a five-year-old girl holding her labia open. What purpose, other than sexual interest, could you have for doing this?*

No, how could you? Dr. Allen mumbled. *They are too small.* (pausing) *I guess if I forced myself to, however, I could.*

The jury returned a verdict in two days. Dr. Allen received a prison sentence of 26 years and 8 months.

The civil lawsuit began shortly thereafter. Had Ms. Allen participated? If not, did she have knowledge of the crimes? Was she, or should she have been, suspicious? What was the psychological impact on the victims?

The Allens had considerable assets. They owned an expensive home and a large preschool. The Allens also had substantial insurance on both properties. Though insurance companies now have riders excluding liability for sexual abuse, policies did not contain them in the 1970s and early 1980s.

Insurance liability, however, does not extend to intentional acts. Even if Dr. Allen's behavior had been intentional, there was still the question of whether Ms. Allen had been complicit, either as a participant or as an enabler. Or had she been a negligent supervisor, failing to prevent a foreseeable harm when her husband took children off the school grounds?

Dr. Allen would tell Ms. Allen, *I'm going to take (so-and-so) for ice cream.* He would then bring the child to their house, where the sexual molestations and child pornography occurred. Ice cream would be purchased on his return to school.

Though accusations of child sexual abuse are often very difficult to prove, amounting to a child's word against that of an adult, the situation at Alicia's Preschool was obviously very different. A large group of children were sexually assaulted, and the crimes were methodically recorded. The truth was in the pictures. Dates, frequencies, and images of the acts were contained in the slides themselves.

While the facts of the molestations were never in dispute, getting children to talk about their feelings for a damages argument in a civil lawsuit was another matter entirely. I played games with them, went for walks with them—whatever it took to gain their confidence—doing the same with their parents and siblings. I also interviewed other significant people in their lives, such as teachers, to get a fuller picture of their psychological functioning. Every child had also been referred to a psychotherapist.

Though many emotions emerged, severe anxiety and depression salient among them, one symptom was especially noteworthy among the victims. Without exception, each child was haunted by the existence of the pornographic slides. Though the police assured the families and children that the slides had been destroyed, this guarantee did little to allay their grief and shame.

The parents were also convinced that the slides had been distributed globally. Pedophiles of that era often exchanged child pornography through UPS, and every parent had a recollection of a UPS truck making repeated pick-ups and deliveries at both the Allen home and the preschool.

The defense attorneys asserted that child pornography is a less traumatic form of sexual abuse than genital penetration. I argued, in deposition, otherwise. Child pornography is devastating not because it is violent or less obtrusive but because it creates an indelible record of a very disturbing and humiliating offense. A child was coerced, defiled, and deceived. That child must thereby contend with the fact that a permanent record of the abuses now exists as well.

Other psychological symptoms were readily apparent consistent with posttraumatic stress disorder— nightmares, school phobia, lack of trust, overeating, academic neglect, and so on. Constant vigilance to cues that could trigger psychological symptoms was evident as well.

Mr. Girardi and Mr. Keese concluded that there was no evidence provided by the children, parents, or teachers that Ms. Allen had been a participant in sexual abuse. She instead had been, they successfully argued, a negligent supervisor who had allowed children to be taken from her preschool without parental consent.

Why did Dr. Allen do it? His confession perhaps provides an answer. He believed, a delusion no doubt, that the sexual molestation, née research, had benefited the children. It was affection, he said. It made them happy (despite evidence of their crying in the slides), and it was a substitute for parental neglect. It wasn't really sex, but a loving gesture instead, because it didn't cross an arbitrary boundary such as penetration.

Was that argument simply a defense strategy used at his criminal trial? Or had that been his mindset throughout the sexual abuse? I believe the latter. People often commit egregious crimes because they have convinced themselves that the behavior is beneficial, inadvertent, or necessary. Those belief systems are often refractory to change. Combined with the fact that a small percentage of men are capable of sexualizing a prepubertal child, that frame of mind goes a long way toward explaining the behavior of pedophiles and their recidivism.

Child pornography is often a masturbatory stratagem for men who are sexually attracted to, or who sexually abuse, children. Such pornography is arousing to pedophiles because it documents adult–child sex. Child pornography is, as well, a device for luring other children into sexually exploitive crimes.

Adult consensual nonviolent pornography, in contrast, is not merely a reflecting mirror into what adults find sexually arousing but also a portal into something more fundamental about sex and the cues that elicit sexual acts, the visual cues in particular. Adult consensual nonviolent pornography is ultimately an ephemeral artifact that can appeal to, or offend, men and women. Child pornography, on the other hand, is a heinous crime against a child.

Hustler Magazine , Inc. v. Falwell

Is sex funny when told by a pornographer—Larry Flynt, for example? Before ending this chapter, I want to introduce the 1988 Supreme Court case of *Hustler Magazine, Inc. v. Falwell*.

Humor has the capacity to defuse or neutralize controversy. Ridicule, in contrast, has the opposite effect. What does that observation tell us about the world of adult pornography and sex more generally?

I am saying that pornography hurts anyone who reads it, garbage in, garbage out, declared Jerry Falwell, the prominent televangelist and cofounder of the Moral Majority. Larry Flynt, the publisher of *Hustler Magazine,* thought otherwise. Falwell, according to Flynt, was ripe for parody.

It began with a liquor advertisement. Campari, an Italian aperitif, had been running an advertising campaign with tongue-in-cheek celebrity interviews spoofing the *first time* interviewees had done "it." Purportedly about sex, the interview eventually revealed that the celebrity was describing, instead, a first-time drink of Campari.

Flynt took this interview format and created a full-page advertisement with the following headline: *Jerry Falwell talks about his first time.* A bottle of Campari, two cocktail glasses, and a photograph of Mr. Falwell looking very contemplative were embedded in the text of the purported interview.

The ad, which ran in the November 1983 issue of *Hustler Magazine* with the disclaimer *parody—not to be taken seriously*, was anything but contemplative. Falwell, the purported interviewee, declared that his first sexual experience had been with his *Mom, in an "outhouse[,]" of all places, and that both* [had been] *"drunk off our God-fearing asses on Campari."* Falwell also confessed to having been so intoxicated that his *Mom looked better than a Baptist whore with a $100 donation.*

Was that ad funny? The readers of *Hustler Magazine* thought so, but Mr. Falwell was aghast and sued Mr. Flynt. The United States Supreme Court, however, unanimously upheld Flynt's right to parody a public figure, gross sexuality notwithstanding. There is a long history of such parodies, and their protection is deemed essential for protecting political debate.

Though incest is a felony crime of universal revulsion, a sexual joke about incest, on the other hand, might be capable of defusing the horror associated with it. Humans seek and appreciate devices that can give respite from the unrelenting tragedies that confront us. Nobody really believed that Jerry Falwell had had sex with his mother. The parody ad was funny because it was so transparently ludicrous.

Conclusion

The fleeting silhouettes of nonviolent, consensual adult pornography that seep through the scrim of litigation history rarely do justice to the complexity of the constitutional issues underlying porn. Overwhelmingly graphic and unseemly in many regards, pornography is nonetheless emblematic of nonconformity, packaged ironically as vibrant tabloid revelry.

The freedom to view consensual, nonviolent adult pornography and to consider the ideas contained therein is fundamental to our constitutional republic, no less so than the choice to inspect a religious text. Though it's easy to trivialize porn, the issues it raises—the freedom of speech, for example—are by no means trifles.

CHAPTER 3:
A Far Cry from the Truth

I know a guy who has an answer for everything. He is a professor of math at UCLA. It didn't matter what I asked him; Bruce Rothschild knew the answer. *I don't know much about this,* he'd say and then dazzle me with his explanation. Before the Internet, Bruce was my Google search.

When the AIDS crisis gathered steam in the early 1980s, the critical epidemiological question was, How bad is this going to get? Bruce and I worked on a simple mathematical model designed to emulate the impact of biological and behavioral cofactors.

I wrote the first draft. Bruce ripped it up.

It wasn't that I had failed to explain our model; I did fine with that. But my language offended Bruce. It was unnecessarily overstated. That had to go.

Mathematics is judged on a 4,000-year timeline, and the field is miserly with praise. Psychology, in contrast, reinvents itself every fortnight and then clamors for the floodlights.

Recognizing that science is best perceived in the rear-view mirror was certainly an important development, but I also wanted something more. I didn't know, however, what I wanted until I stumbled upon the writings of Karl Popper, the philosopher of science.

Falsifiability was Popper's trademark, criticism his sword. Scientific theories prosper either logically or experimentally by surviving attempts to falsify them. Being open to criticism is thus the distinguishing characteristic of science.

Best of all, I liked how Popper dismissed academic disciplines entirely. Psychology, anthropology, biology—they were administrative conceits at best, as was their claim to a preferred methodology. The only thing that mattered to Popper was the problem. Problems drive science and determine methods. Scientists need only concern themselves with attempts to solve problems.

With few exceptions, I never did traditional psychological research again. Problems became my bailiwick, and I employed methods—mathematical models, narrative theories, and constitutional scholarship—that suited the conundrums I grappled with. Though blasphemy to many of my colleagues, this approach made sense to me.

Are multiple one-night stands with condoms riskier than serial monogamy without them? Why is sex so pleasurable? Why don't Americans have constitutionally protected sexual rights? How does a person who is blind experience sexual attraction? Countless other questions arose as well, organizing the output of my career.

After screwing around with sex for more than four decades, I have now found myself asking—as if peering through a glass darkly—what do we *really* know about sex?

Beyond Sound Bites and Fairy Tales

Sex research used to be easy. All it took was a white lab coat, a poker face, and a sex questionnaire. It didn't matter that the results weren't exactly true. They never really are. These were baby steps, a corrective for Bible thumpers.

It soon changed, however. An armory of methods, models, disciplines, and theories materialized. Pornography, abortion, contraception, Viagra, gay rights,

AIDS, and plenty more riveted attention. One thing, nevertheless, remained the same. People lied like hell about sex.

How, then, do we build a science when the fundamental unit of measurement is so imprecise? At what point do we stop ignoring this conundrum? Sex researchers have grown accustomed to an orchestrated veneer that includes cursory measurement and pseudoscientific nomenclature in lieu of accurate description, reproducibility, and laws. Perhaps it's time to wake up and smell the coffee.

The Truth About Lies

It was two kids having sex, or what appeared to be penile–vaginal intercourse. Their pants were down, and they were gyrating in rhythmic fashion.

This video emerged in an expert witness case of mine in Jackson Hole, Wyoming. A fire extinguisher had been set off at the back of an elementary school bus. To investigate, school officials had examined footage from the bus security camera.

I didn't take my pants down, each kid claimed, even when told of the video footage.

I introduce this case to make two points. Human sexuality starts young, and it's private—disguised, clandestine, or distorted.

Many kids engage in explicit sexual conduct well before puberty—mutual masturbation, oral sex, anal sex, penile–vaginal intercourse, and so on. It may not include full penetration, orgasm, or other hallmarks of adult sexual acts, but sex nonetheless happens in a rudimentary form.

In some cases, adults have sexually abused a child, thereby influencing the onset of the child's sexual behavior. This situation is not true for most kids. Sex manifests itself because it feels good. Pleasure is thus the engine that drives the system. It doesn't take a kid long to realize that stimulating the genitals is fun. Rhythmic touching is even better, and once discovering it, kids are hooked.

This is not to say that hormones, evolved reproductive strategies, or cultural pressures don't influence sex—all obviously exert strong effects. But pleasure is the primary feature of the sexual system. The eyes see things, ears hear things, hands grasp things, and genitals feel things—really good things, in fact.

Kids experience sexual attractions, too—quite basic ones, of course, but distinctive nonetheless.

Is it an elementary reproductive strategy? If so, why do gay- identified kids experience it as well? Or is it the embryonic form of sexual affiliation, an unspecified excitement or anxiety about sexual things to come? Either way, it is evident that kids have incipient sex and that they are attracted to the precursors of potential sexual partners.

Then there is the issue of lying: brazen, inadvertent, malicious, time and again.

A number of years ago, I conducted a study that asked college students to keep a two-week sexual diary. When they had finished, students were then asked to recall what they had reported. They couldn't get it right. The frequency of sex went up, and other details were distorted, too. Though many explanations could suffice to explain these results, there was no escaping the implication. Even when keeping a sexual diary for two weeks, it's hard to remember what happens in the bedroom.

Big-time liars exist, too: the John Edwardses (the Democratic vice presidential candidate who lied about his mistress and her pregnancy); the Eliot Spitzers (the governor of New York who hid his extensive use of prostitutes); the cheating husbands, wives, boyfriends, and girlfriends; the sexually abusing priests, Boy Scout leaders, coaches, teachers, police officers, and so on. It's hard not to be suspicious of everything people tell us about sex.

Kinsey realized this. He spent time building rapport before taking sexual histories. Is that why Kinsey discovered a higher percentage of sexual minorities? Even if this result were true, his data were undoubtedly off the mark as well—it's part of the nature of the beast to lie about sex.

The most egregious forms, however, are the lies surrounding criminal acts (e.g., sexual abuse, sexual assault, rape). I see them all the time in my expert witness work. Lies upon lies upon lies.

At some level, however, everyone is a liar—even porn stars. Who hasn't done something embarrassing or shameful, or feared the consequences of a sexual act? Sex may be heaven, but lying about sex is the sure bet.

Which brings me back to sexual pleasure. Much of what has been written about sex—the gene of the month, the dynasty of the apes, Oedipus on fire—would give Rudyard Kipling a run for his money. I prefer instead to begin with the capacity for pleasure. It's observable and a closer fit with *Occam's razor*—the fewer the assumptions, the better.

The body is designed for pleasure—orgasmic delight being foremost—but other erogenous zones exist as well—kissing, for example. Then there is the clitoris. It has no reproductive function. The same is true of female orgasm. Women get pregnant without it.

Pleasure motivates kids to indulge in sex despite their inability to reproduce. Humans then continue their fascination with nonreproductive sex (e.g., oral sex) over the course of a lifetime.

This phenomenon should come as no surprise. A tight, moist orifice (e.g., vagina, mouth, anus) or enclosure (e.g., a lubricated hand) is ideally suited for stimulating a penis. A reproductive prerequisite is not required.

Though the impulse is less pronounced on average, women have similar experiences with sexual pleasure. The vibrator industry thrives accordingly. Bonobo females find a way to capitalize on genital pleasure (e.g., rubbing their genitals together), too. The loss of fecundity in postmenopausal women doesn't eliminate the pleasures of sex, either.

Puberty is a different story. Pleasure then serves two masters: reproduction and nonreproductive acts. Reproduction insures the survival of the species, and nonreproductive sex delivers tangible benefits, too (e.g., joy, bonding, conflict resolution, the feeling of power, tension reduction). The real game-changer, however, is pregnancy. After puberty, sex is no longer a level playing field. Women get pregnant; men don't. Men thus wander blithely, and women proceed with caution.

Are these evolved reproductive strategies whereby men are promiscuous to ensure paternity and thereby pass on their genes while women are highly selective, only picking mates who will ensure the survival of their offspring?

Perhaps. But it's also not the only game in town. After puberty the *costs* of sex are vastly different for men and women. Our problem-solving brains figure this out, and then many factors (personal, peer-related, parental, cultural, evolved) conspire to make women more cautious about sex—certainly regarding reproductive sex—and more choosy about sexual partners.

This is not to say that sex is void of adaptations, a primate heritage, hormonal events, or more. All species are programmed through evolution to maximize reproduction, humans no less so. That fact notwithstanding, I still favor observables: sex starts young and feels great, women get pregnant and men don't, and our problem-solving brains are good at figuring stuff out.

Whether anyone actually engages in sex is another matter entirely. The old joke is that women have a sixth sense. They can tell who is going to get laid tonight. Proximate determinants such as culture, peers, wives and girlfriends, husbands and boyfriends, and so forth thus rule supreme—certainly in the overt manifestation of sex. This is both the power and the vulnerability of our overriding brains. If culture, parents, or peers condemn masturbation, for example, there will be fewer masturbators or incalculable masturbatory guilt. Sex is thus no less hardwired than ephemeral and no less an adaptation than a spur-of-the-moment thing.

Darwin's Love Child

Once upon a time sex was an infinitely malleable behavior. Man, woman, slut, virgin all clocked in from the same source—culture.

Then came the unmasking. Drawing upon the work of the eminent evolutionary biologist George Williams, Don Symons proposed that our sexual psychology (mating patterns, promiscuity, beauty) evolved through natural selection. Symons was careful to emphasize that his premise applied only to adaptations, sexual psychological characteristics that evolved to maximize reproductive success.

Why, for example, are heterosexual men attracted to healthy young women? Is this phenomenon a culturally driven norm? Was it invented by the pornography industry? The world of advertising?

Symons proposed instead that healthy young women are a proxy for fertility. Heterosexual men are attracted to them because men are programmed—through evolution—to know that sexual relations with healthy young women would have the highest probability of reproductive success. Attraction to healthy young women is thus an adaptation.

Whether you agree with Symons in whole or in part is irrelevant. Either way, Symons forever changed the discourse about the nature of human sexuality by catapulting it into the world of natural selection. One can't speak or theorize about sex without recognizing his impact.

Therein lies the problem. Though Symons is a meticulous theorist, his expertise is not endemic in the social sciences, where sex is often treated as a convenient launching pad for adaptation anecdotes.

Experimental biologists have repeatedly demonstrated that evolution can be rapid for some species, occurring even over a couple of years. This finding, curiously, has escaped recognition by many evolutionary sexual psychologists. More importantly, evolved traits— even at the genetic level—can also be nonintuitive covariates of another trait. This observation, too, has failed to make a dent in the sexual psychology mindset.

Take deer mice. Those that live on light-colored sand dunes are lighter in color than those living on the surrounding prairie. Is this phenomenon an adaptation? Lightening up, it was argued, protects mice by making it easier for them to blend into a light-colored dune and thereby avoid detection by airborne predators such as owls.

To add more credence to this story, biologists ultimately discovered the pigment-related gene. This outcome did not, however, answer the fundamental question. Is coloration adaptive—that is, was it naturally selected because it provides a survival advantage?

Rowan Barrett captured Nebraska deer mice living on light and dark ground. He sampled their DNA and marked them for follow-up studies. Then he released them (half light and half dark) into six field enclosures, either sand hills or dark soil nearby. Eventually, Barrett trapped all the captured mice in each enclosure every few months during the next two years. He noted which had survived the onslaught of owls, and he monitored the survivors' genes.

True to form, the dark mice did better on dark soil, and the light mice did better on light sand. Barrett also discovered, interestingly, that many genes unrelated to pigment changed, too—all responding to natural selection—and unrelated to surviving predation. The other adaptations were thought to make the mice healthier or better able to find food.

This research on the rapid course of evolution directly answers questions about the underlying genes. Nonintuitive findings emerged as well.

Now contrast these findings with a recent study by evolutionary psychologists reporting that they, too, have discovered objective support for an adaptation.

Forty-eight college women made fewer phone calls to their dads during ovulation. This finding was purported to be evidence that women avoid reproduction-compromising behaviors, such as inbreeding, during periods of peak fertility because they would reduce reproductive success.

With other primates—chimpanzees, for instance—young females cease to travel with close male kin and experience reduced sexual attraction to familiar males. The primary strategy for avoiding inbreeding, however, is dispersal. Young males remain with the group while young females leave before breeding. The genetic advantages (mitochondrial DNA) of this type of migration have been supported by research as well. Bonobos (another primate) practice a similar type of dispersal, with the same evolutionary benefits.

Some researchers of primates and small mammals, however, believe that sexual dispersal patterns are epiphenomenal consequences of intrasexual aggression, for example.

The question before us now is whether fewer phone calls to dad during ovulation are analogous to any of these findings— migration, dispersal, or intrasexual aggression. Are fewer phone calls to dad a 21st-century analog of avoidant inbreeding? Is examining the phone logs of 48 female college students a reasonable methodology for resolving these questions?

Phantom leaps are common pratfalls on the evolutionary sexual psychology road map, the most flagrant exemplars of which are rape and homosexuality.

According to this spurious logic, early raping protohuman males had more offspring, an occurrence that in turn distributed a raping gene throughout the male genotype. If, however, the frequency of sex increases the probability of conception, rape would be an inimical strategy. Friendship and affiliation would be more effective strategies because they offer substantially more opportunities for sex than horrifying a guileless victim.

Increased sexual aggression from male lizards, for example, has significant adverse effects on females of the species, including reduced survival and fertility rates. The amplified effect of male sexual aggression in fact is a major risk for population extinction among lizards.

Rapists are better understood as merciless thieves who bank on not getting caught. Eliminating rape is thus about catching and severely punishing rapists. Universal empathy for victims also serves prosecutorial goals.

Homosexuality is another controversial topic in evolutionary sexual psychology. Why does homosexuality exist if it has no reproductive benefits?

The evolutionary psychology answer to this conundrum is built on two interrelated principles. The first is Fisher's fundamental theorem of natural selection, whereby organisms strive to maximize their own reproductive success. The limitation of Fisher's theorem is that it can't explain altruistic behavior. If an animal puts itself in danger (e.g., uttering an alarm call) to protect others or if a worker insect foregoes reproduction entirely, neither is striving to maximize its own reproductive success.

Building upon Fisher's fundamental theorem and Sewall Wright's observation that relatives carry replicas of the same gene, William Hamilton proposed a second principle called inclusive fitness. It explains the genetic advantages of altruism among relatives who live in close proximity.

Evolutionary psychology believes that altruism also solves the homosexuality riddle. Homosexuality persists because gay brothers and gay sisters altruistically care for relatives (siblings, nieces, nephews), thereby increasing their own genes' survivability. Since relatives have a high probability of carrying replicas of brother, sister, aunt, or uncle genes, the gay gene is thus passed on to future generations.

It is important to emphasize from the start that a gay gene itself has never been isolated. Dean Hamer and colleagues certainly located a region on the X chromosome that a portion of gay men who had gay brothers shared in common, but that discovery is a far cry from isolating a gene. Since multiple genes determine complex forms of behavior, there is also no reason to suspect that homosexuality—a multifaceted psychological phenomenon—wouldn't fall into that category, if it fell into a category at all.

What if homosexuality as we know it is illusory? In some cultures, for example, only the male "bottom" is labeled gay, not the "top." Other cultures have teenage homosexual rites of passage, after which the males transition into exclusively heterosexual identities.

Women can also have fluid sexual identities—one time gay, one time not. Some prisoners will do it with whoever is willing (or not) and available within the confines of a prison. Bisexuality certainly exists as well.

The nonhuman data are no less inconclusive. Bonobos prefer female–female sex, while some other primates like the male–male kind. Even same-gendered sex can be classically conditioned, in Japanese quail, no less.

I believe evolutionary psychologists have mistakenly invoked homosexuality as a proxy for infertility—as if all homosexuals are loath to reproduce. Oscar Wilde, one of the most famous "homosexual" men of all time—and the most celebrated person ever convicted of sodomy (indecency)—was married and had kids. The critical question for evolutionary sexual psychology should instead be, Why does involuntary infertility persist?

Presuming for a moment that infertility is a genetic trait, why would it persist in human populations? One argument is inclusive fitness—infertile sibs increasing the survivability of their brothers and sisters. That theory is certainly reasonable, but perhaps something else is operative, too.

I call it the *exemption principle*, which is a bastardization of the excision theorem in algebraic topology. Like inclusive fitness, the exemption principle is an exception to Fisher's theorem that helps to explain an anomaly—how a gene or characteristic like infertility could persist even though it doesn't maximize individual or species survival.

Humans are an extraordinarily fertile species. Our real risk is overpopulation. Nonreproducing members of the species certainly have value by increasing the survivability of others, but they also simultaneously have value by keeping population growth in check by not reproducing themselves. The infertile gene still gets passed on through relatives. But it doesn't get eliminated through the machinations of natural selection because it doesn't compromise the viability of the species, hence the exemption.

Humans are also part of a complex ecosystem where population dynamics are critical. What was sexually advantageous for early protohumans when establishing the species is not necessarily advantageous for the 21st-century variety, for whom overpopulation, in combination with climate change and the future of food, is the dominant peril. In the original Malthusian framework, pestilence and war purportedly kept the human population in check. With increased life span, childbirth technologies, medical advances, agricultural innovations, and global diplomacy, the rules of the game are now different. Overpopulation is certainly a risk, and humans have to adjust accordingly— their sexuality included.

Here, perhaps, is where nonreproductive sex comes in: not only infertility but also other forms—oral sex, for example, which does not lead to conception. Besides putting the brakes on population growth, nonreproductive sex fosters intimacy and promotes conflict resolution—all the while imparting pleasure as it goes.

None of this discussion is meant to disparage the painstakingly complex data collection strategies of many evolutionary psychology researchers or minimize the deep thinking that propels the field. It is instead simply an attempt to broaden the evolutionary model that applies to human sexuality.

Darwin, for example, believed that an organ originally designed for one purpose could be converted for an entirely different purpose—a functional shift, so to speak, whereby a swim bladder eventually serves respiration. Darwin also asserted that covariation (whereby unrelated traits could evolve together) could occur in response to natural selection as well.

Darwin's findings are especially important when theorizing about sex—human sexuality included. Though nailing down an adaptation can lend itself to a good story—babysitting gay brothers and sisters, for instance—other evolutionary dynamics deserve equal billing as well.

Besides functional shifts and covariation, there are coadaptations (mutual adaptation), biogeography (how the physical environment influenced evolution), epigenetics (heritable changes in gene activity that are not caused by changes in the gene sequence), polygenic inheritance, and evolutionary interactions with other species, too. The widespread diversity of *hominid genera* is a direct challenge to the linear progression of natural selection.

Collective traits may also have a combined utility. So long as the combined utility is great, an irrelevant or nonfunctional trait may persist in the face of natural selection pressure. Even the much-maligned Lamarkian theory of the heritability of acquired traits has recently proved useful in a very limited domain (ocean warming on tabletop corals). There is thus no reason to rely on simple one- dimensional evolutionary post hoc explanations.

It may not even be necessary to argue that every form of human sexual behavior has a distinct evolutionary advantage. Some sexual behaviors (e.g., oral sex) may persist because they don't have a *disadvantage,* thereby avoiding elimination by natural selection. The extraordinary replicating machines that we are may be able to enjoy a vast array of sexual acts without ever compromising the replication of the species. Perhaps, as noted previously, these nonreproductive sexual acts afford secondary gains that serve the species as well.

What if, instead of being part of a fixed reproductive strategy, the sexes are forever in an evolutionary arms race? In mammalian societies in which a small number of males rule the roost, males kill the infants of their rivals. To overcome infanticide, females started having sex with many males, thereby diluting paternity and eliminating infanticide. Evidence of this relationship is based upon decades of field observations that recorded fluctuating testis size following the repeated evolutionary transitions from infanticide to female sexual promiscuity.

If mating strategies ebb and flow in other mammals, perhaps the same is true of humans. Infanticide has certainly existed in human societies, and there are legal prohibitions against it. The bigger question is whether this evolutionary transition in mating strategies has also occurred in human history. Was there a point where female promiscuity eliminated infanticide? If so, female promiscuity would be as *natural* and fluid as male promiscuity within the appropriate reproductive pressures.

Is there a contemporary example of mutable reproductive pressures? What about birth control pills and vasectomies? They allow both men and women to enjoy multiple sexual partners without reproductive risks. In vitro fertilization—with more than 5 million babies and counting—is yet another example of a reproductive shift. Are these technological advances mere anomalies that can be safely disregarded in favor of the purported underlying evolutionary mechanisms of human reproduction? Or do they herald something else entirely—reproductive pressures capable of modifying gender-specific sexual strategies? Birth control pills and other modern reproductive technologies are certainly furthering egalitarianism. However, whether they are also modifying sexual strategies critical to evolution is another matter entirely.

What about sexual attraction? Is it based on visual cues—hip-to- waist ratio, for example, or male status? Adults who are blind use multiple cues (auditory, tactile, and so on) to make sexual choices. Though hardly surprising since all mammals rely on multicue mating systems, the questions are then whether sighted humans ignore multiple cues and, if they do, what price they pay for doing so. Multicue mating systems are designed by natural selection to increase the benefits of mating choices.

Then there is the brain.

Brainiacs

I like to think of the sexual brain as having two parts, a navigational device and consciousness. The navigational device is a personalized sexual road map, crafted through a dynamic interplay of genotypic and phenotypic input and manifested as a continuously updated GPS that underscores the psychoneurophysiology of sexual pleasure, sexual attraction, and sexual functioning.

Consciousness, however, is another matter entirely. Though road maps are directional (when travel goals are imposed), consciousness is discretionary. Biological and cultural input notwithstanding, the conscious problem-solving brain is ultimately the progenitor of the sexual choices we make. Whether gay, straight, or in-between—or pondering the where, when, or with whom—the capacity to choose and the responsibility of making those choices are the quintessential hallmarks of human sexuality. All the rest—adaptations, cultural values, and psychological dynamics—is simply prologue.

I started toying with this idea in the late 1970s when working on the book *Sarah: A Sexual Biography.* As noted in Chapter 2, a former UCLA student of mine had shared a ghastly story of sexual abuse—incest with her father and stepfather, rape by a stepbrother, and then a history of adolescent prostitution. I never doubted the seismic impact of the trauma, but I also found myself wondering how one rises above it—if at all?

Novelists, poets, and moviemakers nowadays, of course, routinely fictionalize this subject matter, the culture having adapted to the shock of such disclosures. The purported repercussions, however, tend to be much less nuanced than what happens in reality, as if there were a template for the aftermath of sexual abuse—the drug addict, for example, or perhaps the prostitute. In reality, sexual road maps are idiosyncratic; so, too, is the mental processing of trauma. Two people with the exact same tragic antecedents never develop identically. The unique meaning attributed to trauma—rather than trauma itself—best explains the psychological reactions to it. This is especially true of posttraumatic stress disorder.

I call this theory *cognitive-existential.* What initially mattered to me was Sarah's thinking behind the sexual choices she had made. What I wanted to understand was how she had extracted meaning from her experiences and then how she had translated that meaning into a sense of herself in the world, hence the existential part.

After a second review in *The Los Angeles Times,* the usual assortment of curiosities manifested themselves, but more importantly, attorneys throughout the country also began asking me to serve as an expert witness in litigation involving childhood sexual abuse. As noted in the previous two chapters, I've spent countless hours interviewing hundreds of victims of sexual abuse, sometimes over periods as long as five years. Unlike the typical disclosures made to a therapist, these cases were accompanied by an extraordinary amount of supplemental evidence—police reports, collateral witnesses, videotaped confessions, and more. The facts themselves were thus rarely in dispute, making the casework a do-it-yourself lab for thinking deeply about sex. It's been one of the distinguishing characteristics of my professional life.

I worked, for example, on a clergy sexual abuse case in New Haven, Connecticut, involving a troubled 19-year-old named Rusty Vico. Talking to a priest made sense to Rusty—he was devoutly religious—but it was an ambivalent choice at best. Three years previously the same priest had fondled Rusty's genitals.

This time the priest told Rusty—now in the early stage of schizophrenia—to take off his clothes and lie down on a coffee table. Rusty doesn't remember exactly what happened next, but two weeks later he locked himself in a bathroom and sawed his hand off with a fishing knife. *If thine hand offends thee, cut it off,* he heard in his head.

When I met Rusty 30 years later, in a McDonald's, of all places, he said that victims of clergy sexual abuse never make it to heaven. Cutting his hand off was his ticket through the pearly gates.

Then he smiled. Rusty grabbed a cloth necklace from under his shirt. *This is* a *devotional scapula,* he said. *The wearer is guaranteed admittance into heaven when he dies.*

If I knew that, I'd never'ds cut my hand off. Rusty gave me a scapula, too.

Rusty's schizophrenia was obviously a critical factor in the amputation, but this tragedy was comprehensible—at least in terms of understanding his thinking and actions—in the organization of his narrative. It was the thinking and the broader meaning that Rusty assigned to those facts that made his life story come alive.

I worked on a case in Texas, retained by the plaintiff's attorney, involving a 5-year-old girl, Kate, who had been brutally raped. Her 38-year-old mother, Heidi, was in law enforcement, and her mother's boyfriend, Bob, was a 19-year-old former juvenile prisoner. Bob was the rapist.

Hemorrhaging from the assault, Kate had a tear from her vagina to her anus. Bleeding and wrapped in a blanket, she had been brought to the Emergency Room. Rushed into surgery, Kate spent two more days in the hospital before she was eventually returned to her mother. Once she was again at home, Bob had repeatedly raped Kate for 12 more months.

Shortly thereafter, Kate passed a note to a friend in her classroom explaining what was going on at home. A teacher intercepted the note, the police were then called, and Heidi and Bob were arrested and subsequently convicted. In Heidi's videotaped confession, she was asked, *How could you let this happen*? Through a flood of tears, Heidi whispered, *My truck was broken, and Bob fixed it.*

No less remarkable was Kate's commentary. Rage, pity, and shame were conspicuously missing; poise and intelligence were evident instead. The 13-year-old Kate noted, *My past was unfortunate*, *but I have much more life to live*. Though a host of intellectual and psychological factors could be marshaled to explain her reactions, the idiosyncratic rendering of how she sorted out the details and then came to this conclusion was perhaps the most striking thing of all.

Thinking, choosing, and freely acting brains are also the reason why rapists and sex abusers are justifiably abhorred and punished. If this situation were otherwise, there would be no reason to hold people responsible for their sexual acts, whatever they might be. Immunity from culpability and punishment would be singularly credible if only causes outside of our control propelled us forward.

The same might be said of conditioning. Though sexual preferences can be conditioned or modeled by observing others, and pairing stimuli with orgasm makes the linkages even stronger, sex doesn't unfold in a vacuum. Humans continuously process relevant sexual cues. Being hard to resist is not synonymous with the absence of responsibility. Choosing to ignore cues and constraints is a volitional act, the burden of which falls squarely upon our shoulders.

I raise these points once again to emphasize that in a causally determined sexual system—however defined—the notions of free choice and moral responsibility vanish. I instead believe that the factors influencing human sexuality—pleasure, adaptations, culture—are ultimately filtered through human consciousness, the prefrontal cortex in particular. Prefrontal regions of the brain make probabilistic inferences about the propriety and reliability of behavioral choices. That assessment is ultimately the arbiter of sexual acts as well as the dynamic by which we become responsible for our sexual choices.

Some people disagree. Focusing upon the Pleistocene era in particular (beginning 2.6 million years ago and ending 12,000 years ago), they are convinced that we can infer how human sexuality evolved and manifests itself today by imagining the reproductive problems confronting humans of that era, the vicissitudes of Cro-Magnons getting it on, as it were.

Certainly, this is an important consideration, but I am not convinced it gets us any closer to latter-day humans. Though we are designed to maximize reproduction, maximizing reproduction is not a fixed strategy, a Nash equilibrium, so to speak, anchored in the Pleistocene era. Species instead evolve continuously as our environments change and evolve.

Take domestication. Genetic variations—including rapid evolutionary changes—occur when animals are domesticated. In the rabbit, for example, there are many genetic variants evident across the genome, and most of the regulatory regions are related to brain development.

Dogs are even more complex. Morphometric analysis, for example, has provided thousands of measurements of dog skulls and skeletons. Combined with ancient DNA, morphometric analysis can depict domestication in progress, such as wolves changing into dogs. More intriguing yet is the theory that dogs domesticated *themselves* to exploit benefits from humans (e.g., access to carcasses), a development that, in turn, ignited a second phase of domestication, this time by humans, to capitalize on dog skills such as being keen lookouts.

Darwin also believed that humans have been domesticated. Selective breeding for tameness, for example, produces similar side effects in many animals, including smaller brains and facial feminization. Scientists also believe that advanced language and social skills, plus a lengthening of biologic development, accompanied domestication in humans, too. Even the migration of herders, approximately 4,500 years ago, changed the genetic makeup of today's Europeans. Why, then, should we rely upon events of an imagined couple of million years ago when evolution is continuous and so much more complex?

Interactions between the sexes also produce remarkable diversity, the courtship rituals of male birds, for example. On the other hand, courtship, mating, and offspring can have costs, including increased mortality. Even the presence of the opposite sex can reduce fitness. More intriguing yet, merely *perceiving* the opposite sex can increase mortality and shrink an animal's overall size.

Which brings me back to culture. The intricacies of evolution notwithstanding, cultures also put a stamp on human sexuality. The barbaric practice of clitorectomy—or female genital mutilation—in sub-Saharan Africa is an extreme case in point. Culture matters. Choosing a sexual partner has a strong cultural imprint, too. Arranged marriages are fundamentally different from romantic ones. Biogeography is important as well. Humans had sex with their neighbors, the Neanderthals.

Sex by Numbers

When all is said and done, sex researchers are still under the influence of an original sin, poseurs in the game of science having never figured out how to accurately measure sex. Though we craft theoretical castles in the sky and rigorously critique methods, we're a far cry from truth because truth is a far cry from sex.

Why should we expect truth when sexual accountability is nonexistent? Why do we expect honesty when talking about sex with a stranger, social scientist or not? Are we to believe that the forces that inhibit and privatize sex are held in abeyance when social scientists enter the room?

A fundamental activity of a scientist is making measurements. Lab scientists make precision a first priority. Take, for example, microbial contamination or cross-contamination of a cell culture. These are pervasive problems with profound consequences. Lab scientists have thus devised procedures to enhance the accuracy of their measurements—checking characteristics of cell lines, DNA fingerprinting, karyotype analysis, isotype analysis, and so on.

Sex researchers instead rely upon a collective nod and wink. Don't question my flimsy data, and I won't question yours. Even challenges rarely provoke meaningful change. One edifice is dismantled and replaced with a newer version of the same.

These concerns, however, are hardly new. The entire history of personality assessment is devoted to the complexity of constructing valid and reliable measures of psychological responding. But sex researchers can't be bothered with such distractions. A quick and dirty questionnaire is so much easier to use, much better than mucking about—perhaps for decades—with validity and reliability studies. Making matters worse, statisticians have argued that all the social sciences are precarious because of rampant problems with data collection, samples, data entering, the choice of statistics used, the reporting of statistics, the formulation of questions that drive research, and more. Mindless empiricism is no solution, either. Though one could empirically demonstrate that people prefer cupcakes with icing to those without, one is hardly an empirical scientist for doing so.

Radiocarbon dating is a great example of what it takes to achieve accurate measurement. This is a technique for establishing the age of organic materials based on the steady rate of decay of carbon-14. But it also contains a major measurement flaw. Radiocarbon dating assumes that a constant proportion of carbon-14 exists in the atmosphere—something that, unfortunately, isn't true. Tree rings were thus used to approximate atmospheric carbon-14 dating, but that method only worked to a point—the maximum age of trees.

Then Christopher Ramsey and colleagues did the unthinkable. Using sediment from a lake bed in Japan, they pushed back the estimate of the existence of carbon-14 in the atmosphere to 52,000 years.

I've come to believe that in many respects we know more about dinosaurs than we know about human sexuality. We've recently discovered, for example, soft tissue in 75-million-year-old bones and have gotten closer to understanding the proverbial bell-ringers of extinction (meteorites, extreme climate fluctuations, tectonic processes). Are there comparable advances in sex research? Certainly contraceptive and reproductive technologies rank high, as does the advent of Viagra, hormone replacement therapies, and so on. The social side of sex, however, is another matter entirely. If we can't accurately measure sex, we're throwing darts in the dark.

Is there a tipping point between being reserved and being candid about sex? Does moral reasoning play a role? How about trust and rapport—do they make a difference in sexual disclosure? If so, how much? Cherry-picking sexuality studies to publish and relegating null results to the trash heap won't help matters either, regardless of how often we call ourselves an *evidenced-based* science.

End Point

Where does all of this get us? Many readers might have preferred a hefty chapter on all things sexual, the juicy parts of research in particular, or perhaps the science of sexual bliss, sprinkled with Confucian parables. If the data had supported it, I'd have given it a go. But they don't. I am, for better or worse, highly skeptical of the academic world I inhabit.

I do, nevertheless, have some practical advice. Eliminate lying, cheating, assaulting, abusing, and raping. Instill this value in children, and create a system in which reporting sexual violations is routine, and they are appropriately punished. Don't shortchange the fun part of sex, either. Sex is the godhead of humanity. It's protected through honesty and vulnerability. Leave pieties and prejudices at the door, and above all else, strive for love.

This chapter has been about removing veils and eliminating the sacred cows of sex research by getting beyond sound bites and fairy tales, as it were. Theory, measurement, scientific rigor, pleasure, and thinking were highlighted instead. Humility, caution, and skepticism, I believe, will push sex research forward, but only if modesty becomes the new black.

CHAPTER 4

Sexual Rights and Egregious Wrongs

Mr. Eric Butt was incarcerated in a Utah prison. His 5-year-old daughter, Anndee, remembering an episode she had seen on the Discovery Channel, asked her father if he would send her a stick figure cave drawing. Mr. Butt complied and sent one to his wife.

The drawing was never delivered. The State of Utah instead convicted Mr. Butt of distributing obscene material to a minor.

The United States Supreme Court considered *Eric Leon Butt v. Utah* in 2012. I wrote the Amicus Curiae brief. The court ultimately decided not to hear the case, a commonplace occurrence.

Was the picture obscene? It was a rudimentary, anatomically correct stick-figure drawing depicting Mr. Butt and Anndee. The caption said, *I'm going to bite your butt.* Butt jokes were common in the Butt family.

The use of anatomically correct stick-figure drawings to teach kids about sex and how to prevent sexual abuse, published by authorities no less than the United States government, raises obvious questions about Utah's reasoning. If the drawing, for example, had been sketched and possessed within a home rather than drawn in and sent from a prison, would it still be obscene? Did Mr. Butts have the right to provide information about sex to his daughter? If not, where do sex education rights reside?

Parents obviously have a right to teach their kids. They have rights to free speech, too. There is, however, no constitutional protection for obscene material, including, apparently, an anatomically correct stick-figure drawing. In a culture that doesn't recognize putative sexual rights, only the right to privacy, the chance of governmental incursion is that much greater.

The Right to Privacy

Privacy is neither the scabbard of sex nor its safeguard. Demanding powerful sexual rights that can limit governmental gainsay of adult consensual choice is a much better alternative. Masturbation, oral sex, contraception, interracial marriage, same-gendered sex, and abortion have all suffered from capricious governmental crusades.

A fundamental right is a right that has been enshrined in the U.S. Constitution—the freedom of speech, for example. Fundamental rights also elicit judicial deference when conflict arises between an established liberty (e.g., speech) and governmental incursion (e.g., censorship).

The right to privacy, however, is not a fundamental right. Cobbled together in 1965, it was designed to protect married couples making contraceptive decisions in the privacy of their homes. Subsequently broadened and extended to unmarried heterosexual partnerships and pregnant women, the right to privacy nonetheless left sexual minorities out in the cold. That situation changed in 2003, when the Supreme Court finally acknowledged in *Lawrence v. Texas* that adult sexual minorities had privacy rights in the bedroom, too.

Lawrence did not create a fundamental right to sodomy—or any other sexual right, for that matter. *Lawrence* merely championed the benefits of emotionally durable and intimate relationships. Gay marriage (*Obergefell v. Hodges*) extended this logic as a resilient symbol of equality. Sexual rights themselves, however, were held in abeyance, as if sexual identity were peripheral to the sexual choices made.

The Ninth Amendment

How can *real* sexual rights be assured? The answer is the Ninth Amendment: *The enumeration in the Constitution of certain rights shall not be construed to deny or disparage others retained by the people.* Without sex there would be no people, and without people there would be no rights. Sexual rights are thus deeply rooted in the bedrock of the rights retained by the people.

The hurdle is the judiciary. Judges have conspired to eliminate the Ninth Amendment through ridicule and neglect. This development is especially ironic given the Ninth Amendment's formative history.

Individual freedom from the oppressive powers of the state was the ideological foundation of the American Revolution. When it came time to ratify the Constitution, however, considerable debate emerged. Anti-Federalists wanted a bill of rights. State constitutions had them; they were essential for insuring individual freedoms.

Federalists argued otherwise. Enumerating a bill of rights would empower the government to usurp individual rights not spelled out beforehand.

James Madison, a coauthor of *The Federalist Papers,* brokered a compromise. To satisfy the anti-Federalists, he duly created the Bill of Rights, which conformed to the freedoms protected in state constitutions. To mollify Federalists, he included the Ninth Amendment. The Ninth Amendment was the repository of those natural rights not formally enumerated.

Thomas Paine once declared, *A long habit of thinking a thing wrong . . . gives it a superficial appearance of being right, and raises at first a formidable outcry in defense of custom.* This statement is true, no doubt, about sexual rights, too, customarily exercised through choice, the right to choose procreation being no less a right than choosing not to procreate.

Adult consensual sexual rights (the partners we choose, the activities we prefer, the ideas we read, and so on) would still be open to judicial scrutiny and possible restriction, of course, but the government would have to demonstrate a compelling State interest to justify any abridgement and then would have to undertake it in the least restrictive manner.

Bowers v. Hardwick and *Lawrence v. Texas*

Should sodomy be a fundamental right? A close reading of *Bowers v. Hardwick* and *Lawrence v. Texas* can perhaps resolve this conundrum.

In some respects, this is a highly unusual method for evaluating a constitutional right. Constitutional rights normally evolve as an aggregate of multiple judicial decisions. Supreme Court cases are thereby scrutinized at length in order to build theoretical principles or to craft theoretical leverage for overturning a well-entrenched precedent. The objective herein, however, is to change the rules of the game. The Ninth Amendment is invisible in plain sight, and sexual rights are deprived accordingly.

The right to privacy is a volatile compromise for sexual freedom fostered by a branch of the government (the judiciary) that has a dismal record of protecting sexual rights. If sex is a right retained by the people and protected by the Ninth Amendment, the rationale for embracing the right to privacy, which simultaneously repudiates Ninth

Amendment claims, is duplicitous at best. Perhaps the two aforementioned cases will make this point clearer.

The first case began in 1982. Michael Hardwick was a 28-year-old gay man living in Atlanta, Georgia. He was cited for taking a beer from a bar and drinking it in public. Hardwick paid a fine, but he failed to appear in court. An arrest warrant was issued, and a police officer went to Mr. Hardwick's apartment. After entering the bedroom, the officer found Mr. Hardwick having oral sex with another man. Both men were arrested for the crime of sodomy.

The district attorney, however, had no interest in the case; both men were consenting adults acting in the privacy of the home. A federal district court also dismissed the case, and the Eleventh Circuit Court of Appeals ruled that the statute itself violated Hardwick's constitutional rights.

Michael Bowers, Georgia's attorney general, nevertheless believed otherwise. His decision led to the Supreme Court case *Bowers v. Hardwick*.

The Georgia sodomy law didn't discriminate by sexual orientation. But enforcement was another matter entirely. The conviction of a gay man, for example, could carry 20 years in prison. Georgia also criminalized adultery. However, that fact didn't stop Michael Bowers from having an extramarital affair during the course of the trial.

Bowers made several arguments in *Bowers v. Hardwick.* A prior 1976 case, *Doe v. Commonwealth's Attorney,* had upheld Virginia's sodomy laws. Bowers wanted the case applied to Georgia. He also believed that sodomy had been condemned throughout American history as *an unnatural lust* that was *morally wrong.*

Lawrence Tribe and Kathleen Sullivan, Hardwick's lawyers, thought differently. Georgia's statute, they asserted, contradicted the Supreme Court's flexibility in interpreting the right to privacy for nonprocreative acts such as the use of contraceptives (i.e., *Griswold v. Connecticut*). No secular state interests (e.g., protecting minors), they noted, supported the Georgia sodomy statute, either.

The Supreme Court wasn't persuaded. In a close 5 to 4 vote, the Georgia sodomy statute was upheld. Chief Justice Warren Burger lowered the boom. Sodomy, he said, was worse than rape *and a crime not fit to be named.*

Seventeen years later sodomy was reprieved in the Supreme Court case *Lawrence v. Texas.*

In 1998, Texas residents Robert Eubanks and Tyron Garner helped their friend John Lawrence move into a new apartment. Later that evening Eubanks and Garner got into a fight. In a fit of rage, Eubanks called the police saying there was a black man in the apartment *going crazy with a gun.* Based upon Eubanks's urging, the police entered the bedroom where Garner and Lawrence were having sex. Both men were arrested under the rarely enforced Texas sodomy law.

In a 6–3 decision, the Supreme Court concluded that *Bowers* hadn't done justice to the constitutional right to privacy while simultaneously violating the Fourteenth Amendment's due process guarantees and liberty more generally. Though the *Lawrence* decision was certainly an extraordinary milestone and an unequivocal reason for celebration, Paul Smith, Lawrence's attorney, also gave credence to criminalizing other forms of consensual sexual behavior—adultery, for example.

Why were other consensual sexual rights sacrificed while gay rights to privacy were being defended? An LGBT identity is not merely an accoutrement that is attached to intimate attractions and behaviors but, instead, is the very opposite. The intimate attractions and behaviors define *LGBT*. The right of consenting adults to make choices in relationships void of tangible harm is liberty itself. This fact is true for monogamy no less than for homosexuality. To cast other sexual rights into the fire to protect LGBT privacy rights is shortsighted at best.

Justice Kennedy, who wrote for the majority in *Lawrence v. Texas*, also believed that sodomy should not be a fundamental right. Advocating for sodomy, he said, demeaned the LGBT community, *just as it would demean a married couple were it said marriage is simply about the right to have sexual intercourse.*

Perhaps that's true, but a sanitized correlate of sex is hardly a tenable rationale for presuming that protecting sodomy is intrinsically demeaning. Venerating sodomy as a fundamental right may also be an idealized goal.

Referring to Justice Stevens's dissent in *Bowers*, Justice Kennedy also reintroduced the following: *[I]ndividual decisions by married persons . . . concerning the intimacies of their physical relationship, even when not*

intended to produce offspring, are a form of "liberty"
protected by the Due Process Clause of the Fourteenth
Amendment.

That is no doubt a well-articulated sentiment, but liberty might be better served when adult consensual sexual choices are protected through the Ninth Amendment and thereafter extended to the states through the Equal Protection and Due Process clauses. Failing to champion sexual rights has repeatedly resulted in criminal penalties for practitioners of nonconforming sexual acts—adultery being an obvious example, but apparently drawing anatomically correct stick-figures, too.

Adulterers are legion, openly so or not. American Presidents, judges, cabinet members, governors, members of Congress, religious leaders, celebrated artists, and athletes have all wandered down this path. The underlying rationale for these choices, however, is still disregarded in the 23 states where adultery remains illegal. Perhaps bigamy and polygamy are better examples. What is the moral rationale for criminalizing simultaneous marriages? Bigamy and polygamy are largely equivalent to marital infidelity. A simultaneous marriage, however, more definitively challenges the two-person matrimonial ideal.

Interracial and same-gendered marriages were rendered illegal for yet another variant on this theme, whereby white women are reserved for only white men, and marriage is a heterosexual covenant. At what point does the pursuit of happiness override the state's power to criminalize marriage, however conceived?

Masturbation is an obvious right retained by the people, one would think, yet sex toys are criminalized in several states. The Eleventh Circuit Court of Appeals, for example, upheld Alabama's ban on vibrators because the law was deemed to represent the legitimate goal of *discouraging prurient interests in autonomous sex.*

Adult consensual incest is another matter entirely. Kin recognition genes and familiarity during child rearing purportedly drive the incest taboo. The taboo exists because incest has the power to psychologically harm participants. Tangible harm to participants is never a legitimate basis for a sexual right or the grounds for decriminalizing a sexual crime.

Behind Closed Doors

I believe that a right to privacy is neither an appropriate nor a particularly solid basis on which to establish rights to sexual behavior. Privacy is not synonymous with sex. It's an allegorical door behind which people do *stuff,* often reduced to detritus and haphazardly defined and redefined over decades. The freedom to make sexual choices is instead the determinative right, not the lock on the door. As Justice Blackmun poignantly noted in his dissent to *Bowers v. Hardwick*:

> *Only the most willful blindness could obscure the fact that sexual intimacy is a sensitive, key relationship of human existence, central to family life, community welfare, and the development of human personality. . . The fact that individuals define themselves in a significant way through their intimate sexual relationships with others suggests, in a Nation as diverse as ours, that there may be many "right" ways of conducting those relationships, and that much of the richness of a relationship will come from the freedom an individual has to choose the form and nature of these intensely personal bonds.*

Faculty–student romance is one of the many ways in which intensely personal bonds emerge among consenting adults. Nevertheless, a sizable number of universities now want to stop it. Falling in love or lust with a student can be hazardous to a professor's health (and employment).

Whether a campus romance should be encouraged or prohibited is secondary to the more fundamental question of whether the *choice* to engage in a campus romance should be protected or precluded. The choice is the determinative right, certainly in consensual relationships void of tangible harm. Capricious standards of decorum are something else entirely.

Power imbalance and conflict of interest underlie the current prohibitions. Doctors, however, date nurses; lawyers date paralegals; directors date actors; and judges date their clerks. Requiring full parity in power as a requisite to romance is unnecessarily extreme. If parity were required, religion, race, gender, and income would be decisive, too.

Such a requirement is wholly unnecessary. Conflict-of-interest principles should be used instead when academic evaluations arise. Judges disclose potential conflicts of interest that are remedied through recusal. Medical researchers disclose sources of funding. If professors and students are old enough to engage in intimate relationships, they're old enough to disclose them. Finding alternative ways of achieving independent academic evaluations is undoubtedly a better corrective than terminating professors' employment or trampling on the rights of consenting adults.

It has been argued that the potential partner with less power in the workplace, or in an educational setting, is at a disadvantage in deciding whether to consent or even in recognizing potential complications. The condescension of the latter concern aside, differences in power are widespread and in the foreseeable future will be inevitable. Rather than the stark prohibitions favored today, policies and norms informed by the nuances of such relationships and by an understanding of human sexual attractions more generally would more sensibly serve both regulation and respect.

Sex between a therapist and client, however, is something else again. Therapy works because of the professional distance between clients and therapists.

Professional distance is essential for transference, whereby the client can transfer feelings upon the therapist, who in turn can embody the better side of each projection. One of the critical reasons that professional organizations and the law penalize therapist–client sex as both a breach of professional responsibility and fraud is that it eliminates the possibility of transference.

Besides avoiding situations of power imbalance and conflict of interest, universities want to minimize their vulnerability to civil lawsuits. What better way to distance oneself from professor–student romance gone awry than to exclude it entirely on a college campus?

When universities become wardens of romantic alignments, they become guardians of intimacy more generally, hardly a legitimate role for academia. The arrangement is expedient, perhaps, but the right to think, choose, and judge freely is the lifeblood of liberty. Personal autonomy and internal self-regulation are impossible without it. We choose whom we love, and in the best-case scenario, we love whom we choose.

The Kids Are All Right

What about kids? Are they sexual rights holders, too? Does the pursuit of happiness entitle minors to sexual liberties? What about sexual pleasure? Sexual pleasure is the primary reason that humans of all ages engage in some form of sex.

If minors have sexual rights, whose liberties prevail when rights collide, those of parents or children? Can we protect children from sexual harm without usurping their potential sexual rights?

If sex—starting with masturbation—feels great and is void of tangible harm, should kids have discretionary choices in how to express their burgeoning sexuality? Or is childhood sexuality forever subsumed under parental control, irrespective of its psychological value to kids?

In humans, the divergence of reproductive and nonreproductive sex is striking. Essentially free of the hormonal regulation of sexual desire, adult human females, unlike many other adult female mammals, can—and do—engage in sex at any time in their menstrual cycle, irrespective of fertility status. Sexual pleasure is not dependent on fecundity, either. Postmenopausal women and prepubescent children of both sexes also experience sexual pleasure, but neither is capable of reproducing.

As puberty unfolds, the drive for sexual pleasure is intensified; the aim shifts from purely self-pleasuring to the consummation of reproductive-like activities. Though evident in both genders, it is especially noticeable in post-pubertal males, with the increasing emphasis on orgasm and ejaculation. Sexual opportunities and risks also arise, and sexual exploration is amplified. The fundamental question, then, is whether kids have legal rights to act upon this urge.

In re Gault: A Cautionary Tale

For all the power of *In re Gault* (1967) to establish legal rights for kids, it's important to keep in mind that the case itself was about sex: a phony phone call gone awry.

The backdrop was beyond regrettable; it involved a punitive juvenile system that justified sending kids to an isolated desert prison in Arizona (Fort Grant) that was notorious for physical and sexual abuse. The judges were scurrilous, the kids didn't have advocates, the sentences were indeterminate, and Fort Grant was extraordinarily punitive.

Gerald Gault had come into contact with the Arizona juvenile system twice before; the infractions had been obscure, and probation was the result. The third time, however, was different. The 15-year-old Gault was sent on June 15, 1964, to Fort Grant to serve an indeterminate sentence.

Gault had been accused of either making or listening to (the details were never resolved) an indecent phony phone call to a Ms. Ora Cook. There was no record of the call or a transcript, either. The presiding judge simply ruled that the purported phone call had been obscene and that Gerald was *habitually dangerous*.

Though Gerald admitted to having made *silly* phone calls in the past, he asserted that he never made the call to Ms. Cook. Instead, a friend of his had made it from Gerald's home. *Are your cherries ripe? Do you have big bombers? Do you give any away? Do you have a big, long prick?* is what his friend had said.

Gault was not allowed to have legal representation or expert witnesses, and he was unable to confront his accuser. If Gerald had been an adult who was judged guilty of making an obscene phone call, the maximum sentence would have been 60 days in jail and a $50 fine.

Though the Supreme Court ultimately confirmed Gault's Fourteenth Amendment rights and the constitutional rights of kids more generally, the broader implications of the case are still relevant today. How do we protect teenagers in the 21st century when sexting, phonication, and other intimate sexual acts exist?

Designing sex education that teaches kids how to protect themselves from sexual harm while simultaneously heralding the benefits of sexual pleasure would be a monumental change in public health policy. Acknowledging the sexual rights of kids would help enormously, too, as would corresponding changes in the laws that relate to teenage sexuality. The goal, ultimately, is to foster teenagers' making informed and developmentally relevant decisions, affirmative consent among them, appropriate for sexuality today.

Happiness

If we protect kids from sexual harm to eliminate excessive trauma, what is the corresponding rationale for sexual rights?

Sex has been denied, in one form or another, to women, to masturbators, to those seeking birth control, to those who enjoy pornography, to interracial couples, to gays and lesbians, to the developmentally disabled, to the severely mentally ill, and so on. Why should kids be any different?

The answer is that they're not. They deserve the pleasure and happiness that sex provides just as much as women, masturbators, family planners, and others do. Why not let kids cherish the idyllic joys that blossom in the absence of adult pressures and responsibilities, including the thrill of sexual exploration? To better protect that privilege, it must be elevated to a right, the pursuit of happiness in particular.

Happiness is an obvious choice because there is a long-standing philosophical tradition that has informed governments, including that of the United States. Locke's Second Treatise is a case in point. At the heart of Locke's argument is the premise that a "social compact" is created between the people and their government. Though some individual rights are necessarily relinquished for the collective good, the people nonetheless retain their inviolable natural rights, the pursuit of happiness being fundamental among them.

Thomas Jefferson formalized the Lockean perspective in the Declaration of Independence. The pursuit of happiness, he believed, is a self-evident truth. James Wilson, a Constitutional Convention delegate, went a step further. Happiness, he believed, *is the first law of government.*

If happiness is equated with pleasure and if pleasure is fundamental to sex, then happiness and sex are inexorably linked. Governments, therefore, have a duty to respect the pleasures of their citizens, sexual freedom being one of them. Since the Constitution safeguards liberty and facilitates the pursuit of happiness, it's also the conduit for protecting sexual freedoms.

The big leap, however, is to extend this logic to kids. Adults have a broad range of sexual liberties, but by what justification should this be expanded to children?

Kids deserve pleasure as much anyone does. The question, then, is what the risks are. Unwanted pregnancy comes to mind; sexually transmitted infections and emotional upheaval do, too.

If sex brings joy and happiness, kids are going to find ways to express it, regardless of the complications. Teaching them how to avoid or minimize the risks of sex is a judicious strategy best achieved, as repeatedly noted throughout this book, through comprehensive sex education.

Masturbation is evident by the age of three, and the pleasure clock is ticking well in advance of puberty. If happiness vindicates sexual rights for kids, providing effective sex education is the only way to prepare them for age-appropriate sexual exploration.

CHAPTER 5:

Crying 4 Kafka and Then There's LOVE

I started composing songs when I was 57 years old. I wrote lyrics, monuments to suffering and tenacity, or collages of voices, largely my own; then I wrote rudimentary music, on either a slide guitar or piano. Though I dabbled in instruments as a kid, it took four more decades before the musician rolled in.

In the third chapter I mentioned a case about a 5-year-old girl who had been brutally raped by her mother's 19-year-old boyfriend. The mother was in law enforcement. I had a similar case involving a North Dakota stepfather who had sexually terrorized his stepdaughter. A chorus materialized: *Fuck Mom, Fuck Dad, Fuck all the memories I never had. Fuck honor, Fuck obey, Fuck the wrath of judgment day.* "Fuck Mom/Fuck Dad" is now entombed as a Crying 4 Kafka song. I'm the lead singer and the lyricist of the band (crying4kafka.com). The music is Americana Desolation punk rock.

"Fuck Mom/Fuck Dad" is hardly the first song to juggle provocative imagery with an explicit, disturbing message, Billie Holiday's "Strange Fruit" being the exemplar:

Southern trees bear a strange fruit. Blood on the leaves and blood at the root. Black body swinging in the Southern breeze. Strange fruit hanging from the poplar trees.

Initially performed in 1939, "Strange Fruit" was a scathing indictment of lynching at a time when White America had not yet fully embraced the cause, perhaps distracted instead by the homilies of Mammy and crew in *Gone With the Wind.*

I soon expanded my song-writing palate to include broader social issues, "Give Sodomy a Chance"—with a corresponding article I wrote with Linda Williamson for *The LA Weekly*—being a case in point:

Byron White, uptight, dynamite, distort, last resort, a Tony on his knees. Jack off, Jack shit, Brad Pitt, Juliette, John

Rawls, natural rights, Canaanites, and acolytes. It's sodomy, it's sodomy, it's sodomy. Give sodomy a chance.

Religion permeates the Crying 4 Kafka oeuvre as well, most conspicuously in two set pieces. The first was a nonintuitive pairing of Crying 4 Kafka with a traditional gospel choir (Mama Pat's Inner Light Gospel Choir) in a performance called *The Sacred & the Profane.* The second project was a musical I wrote (the music was composed with Robin Finck of Nine Inch Nails) titled *The Saint of Fucked-up Karma.* These projects paired overarching psychological motifs with the sonic power of punk. This effort was fully realized in *The Saint of Fucked-up Karma.*

The title is not gratuitous. The story was true (it was one of my expert witness cases) and overwhelmingly fucked up. It involved a police officer caught in the act of raping a 13-year-old boy. It got worse from there. Though the details are true, the names and places are not.

The first scene is below.

Scene 1

Dr. Frank Matthews (Begins his monologue about Porter Jones):

People tell me that I'm a saint for getting involved in these cases. I've never seen it that way. I'm just better at staying detached. It's a blessing—and a curse. (Pauses)

His name was Porter Jones. He was 13 years old. His mother, Dolly, was a prostitute; his father, Jake, was a bank robber who had OD'd on heroin soon after he got out of jail.

Dolly was done. Done with dope. Done with bank robbers. Done with Johns. She had moved to a tiny town near Sedona, Arizona, to get away from it all. She thought she had it made when a friendly cop, Tim Tully, took an interest in her son.

(**Dr. Matthews** acts this part out:)

How old are you?

13

That's close enough. Come on! Want to join the Police Explorers? Ya get a uniform, a badge. Teach you to shoot a gun. You ever shot a gun? Fun as hell!

No! But yeah! said Porter.

Three months go by. Porter is in the Explorers, and Tim Tully lavishes Dolly with gifts, a laptop, all kinds of stuff.

Then one night Tully asks Dolly:

(**Dr. Matthews** acts this part out:)

Hey, I'm having a barbecue. Next Friday night. We got tri-tip. We're gonna ride ATVs. My old girlfriend'll be there. Can Porter come? It'll be great! He can spend the night.

Dolly thinks, Sure, that's fine; he's a cop.

Tim Tully has the barbecue, they eat tri-tip, they ride the ATVs, but at ten thirty, Tully's old girlfriend leaves.

Sixteen miles later her car breaks down. Tully's house is closer than Flagstaff, so she has it towed back to his home.

Something's not quite right. Sheets are covering the windows. She uses her key to open the front door and walks inside.

Right there on the couch Tim Tully is raping Porter Jones.

Tully jumps up. Grabs his gun. Puts it to her head.

She WAILS. Just WAILS.

He puts the gun to his own head. She WAILS even louder.

Tully throws down the gun, calls his department chief, and confesses.

There are three distinct arcs to this musical. The story of Porter, Dolly, and Tim Tully comprise the first arc. The second arc explores the impact of working on cases that involve deplorable crimes. Is Dr. Matthews, for example, still capable of intimacy in his personal life? Keely, his girlfriend, is the device for exploring this question.

The third arc, no less important than the first, explains how Dr. Matthews became involved in this work— not merely the referrals, but how he learned to thrive therein. The second and third arcs are evident in Scenes 2 and 3 below.

Scene 2

Keely: Do you ever get burned out?

Dr. Matthews: What do ya mean?

Keely: Your crazy childhood. The world of trauma?

Dr. Matthews: I'd beware of pity.

Keely: Pity? It's not pity. It's concern. Your life is

enshrined in grief. (Pauses) I know you're fighting for something. Who could miss that? But it all gets mixed up in a twisted kind of way.

Dr. Matthews: I give to these people.

Keely: Your cases. But not to me. Or us.

Dr. Matthews: I see it differently. You thrive on hope. I don't. I don't believe in soul mates. Marriages made in heaven. I can't imagine how any of those things could yield happiness. I want none of it.

Keely: What's wrong with soul mates?

Dr. Matthews: Nothing. Nothing. I just don't believe in them. I look around. Everyone is falling in or out of love. I'm done with it.

Keely: That's depressing.

Dr. Matthews: Things I do, or try to do, are done because I think they're right. It's gotta feel right. Marriage is a crapshoot. I don't like to gamble.

Keely: Is it right between us?

Dr. Matthews: Definitely! Definitely!

Keely: Then why'd you disappear? For three weeks? No calls. Nothing!

Dr. Matthews: I had no choice. I keep telling you that. I had no choice. This case . . .

Keely: You're always on cases.

Dr. Matthews: Not like this one. Cop raping a kid. Can you imagine? Mother is a prostitute. He needed help.

Keely: We need help.

Dr. Matthews: That cop knew exactly what he was doing. This family had billboards on their backs: ***WOUNDED BIRDS.***

Keely: I don't doubt any of that. But it's beside the point. We're a sinking ship. We deserve better.

Dr. Matthews: We're not sinking. Just because I don't feel the way you do doesn't mean that I care any less. (Pauses) You're an artist. You're always seeing things differently. (Pauses) I never know what to do. Keep talking or go for a walk. (Pauses) It's not for the lack of trying. I just never know what to do. I can't figure it out.

Scene 3

Dr. Frank Matthews (Begins a monologue about his childhood):

I was in a terrible accident. I was eight years old. (Lifts his shirt to show the scar.) Fifty stitches. The scar runs from below my belly button to my rib cage, and then it turns right, toward my back. It looks like a jagged lowercase *r*. Imagine it on an 8-year-old. And angry red.

I was standing on a five-foot ledge. I slipped and fell to the concrete below and was knocked unconscious. Another kid fell, too. His knees landed in my stomach. I was dead, or so he thought. He ran away.

When I woke up, I crawled home on both arms, dragging my body behind me, blood dripping from my mouth.

It freaked the hell out of my mother. An ambulance was called, and it took me to Saint Agatha's Hospital. The Emergency Room doctor looked like Sherlock Holmes— not the new actor, but the old one, Basil Rathbone. He was holding an enormous needle.

Frank, he whispered, *you won't feel a thing.*

I didn't.

But I did remember what my father said to me in the ambulance.

You know what the FUCK this is going to cost me?!

Run, Frank, run is all I could think.

Though perhaps it's hard to imagine how this case could have gotten worse, the final scene is also included herein. The music, no less than the story itself, is a fitting destination for an Americana Desolation punk rock band.

Scene 14

Dr. Matthews (Completes his monologue about Porter Jones):

Four years after Porter got out of federal prison, I got a call from a public defender in Albuquerque, New Mexico. Her name was Alba Woods. She asked me if I knew Porter.

(Dr. Matthews acts out the phone call:)

Dr. Matthews: *Yeah. I know him.*

Alba Woods: *He says he was sexually molested by a police officer. Is that true?*

Dr. Matthews: *Yeah. I got all the paperwork.*

Alba Woods: *Would you be willing to tell that to a jury?*

Dr. Matthews: *Why a jury?*

Alba Woods: *Porter Jones has been arrested for a terrible, terrible crime. He kidnapped and raped a 10 year-old girl. Will you please, PLEASE, tell the jury that he did it because of that cop?!?*

Dr. Matthews (loudly): *NO! I'm not going to do that! No way. That card has been played! It's done!! I can't tell you how many times we bailed him out of Juvi. And the misery and heartache of watching him blow* *through the money—only to end up in prison for armed robbery.*

This guy thinks he's immune from punishment. He's on his own. I'm done. No agonized tributes to redemption. This is about accountability! Porter is on the hook for this one!

Dr. Matthews (Looking directly at the audience): Porter Jones was convicted and given a 100-year sentence without parole.

Witnesses saw him kidnap the little girl off the street. The police immediately gave chase. Up and down a windy mountain road. Porter is driving so fast that he goes off a cliff and rolls down into a ditch. Police don't realize it at first; they keep on driving.

Nobody is hurt. Porter climbs out of the car. It's real quiet. He thinks he's home free. He then rapes the little girl in the upended car. Can you believe that?

A year's worth of documentary filmmaking by Verité TV followed thereafter. Like most documentaries, however, it was never finished. Crying 4 Kafka then moved on to yet another project, the CD *Humbled by the King of Porn.*

As noted in Chapter 2, I served as the expert witness for Knight-Time Entertainment. Though the issues were gripping, Mr. Knight, Mr. Dreiser, and Mr. Knight's girlfriend were no less conspicuous. The intent of Crying 4 Kafka's CD was not to condemn or extol pornography but instead to shed light on Mr. Knight and his peculiar world.

The title song, "Humbled by the King of Porn," is a character study of a man who fashioned himself as the Fisher King of erotica. The chorus of this song captures the odd interplay between Mr. Knight's thinking and his behavior:

Casting pearls before the swine, contempt so very crystalline. We were whores, or so he said, as he climbed into bed.

Action camera so very quick. No more scruples with these tricks. Left to wear that crown of thorns. Humbled by the King of Porn.

Why, the reader may now be asking, is Crying 4 Kafka included in a book on sex?

Academics have a habit of behaving like Cheshire cats, tossing off bon mots to adoring acolytes. I'm loath to play that role. Composing music is a viable medium for addressing the issues I wrestle with, including the deplorable cases I've worked on. Crying 4 Kafka may well be off point, but if so, it's an honest mistake, an attempt to broaden an unnecessarily narrow bandwidth so well ingrained in academia.

And Then There's Love

It seemed fitting to end this book with love. Music is a natural segue, and sex begs the question. What is this funny thing called love?

Love comes in various formats—romantic; parent–child; and affection for people, places, and things as well as graded—e.g., supreme, intermittent, middling, and barely sufficient. Ephemeral and episodic come to mind, too, and let's not forget unending.

The real trick, then, is to say something about love that is simple, nuanced, and authentic but that neither confirms the obvious nor corrects the ridiculous, as if disregarding nonsense is a major achievement in and of itself. If a psychologist persists in believing that parents are loved because they feed their infants or are hated in the aftermath of Oedipal struggles, why give such balderdash credence by spending countless hours dismantling it? Max Beerbohm got it right when he remarked how distressed he felt with his failure *to keep up with the leaders of thought as they pass into oblivion.*

I'm also partial to parsimony, wondering if there's really something new to say about love and, if so, hoping that it can be said with economy. Humans are, of course, dependent upon love as children, and the lack of love is disastrous for kids and adults alike. Pair bonding assuredly matters, too, though the adhesion can be conspicuously frail. The latter point makes me wonder if we must forever leverage prudence to accommodate the endless permutations of how love can go asunder.

This is not to minimize the extraordinary power of love. It is, instead, to note that the experience of love is crucial, not the casting about for love's illusive thumbprint. Neurotransmitters notwithstanding, it is the personal world we understand and construct based on a collection of life experiences and fueled by the underlying biological and cultural machinery that is the ultimate arbiter of love.

Chance matters, too. There are no guarantees, and deplorable examples of unloving are ubiquitous. Though I shower my wife and kids with fervent expressions of love, I'm nonetheless a realist. My professional life has been devoted to studying egregious harm often delivered in the guise of love. I'm not even sure that we have the cognitive capabilities for correctly labeling and understanding love— let alone have an adequate language for defining it. Might it be better to shift our energies from trying to define love to recognizing and promoting instead the fundamental human right to experience emotional joy and bliss as a proxy for love?

Perhaps we struggle with grasping love because it is an abstraction. We feel it and attest to its depth, but neither action guarantees a solid foundation. What we understand about love simultaneously reveals what we don't understand about it, as if the axioms of love forever harbor their own logical contradictions. Why is love, for example, so often short-lived? Why do we fall out of love? Why do so many marriages fall apart? Why are parent-child relationships so often fraught with struggle? Why doesn't love always last?

Psychologists pretend to know answers, but I think logical contradictions are fundamental to love, as if love can never prove its own consistency. Love may be beautiful, and its light blinds us, but its deepest problems arise out of its own mysteries, the greatest of which are the contradictions that are essential to it. Though this may sound like the ramblings of a malcontent, I am by no means immune to the power of love. But is that fact sufficient to give me insight into it? Unloving surrounds us. Is it because a vast majority of the world's population hasn't figured this truth out? Or are some of us simply lucky to have stumbled onto the durable kind of love that is then infused with selfless devotion?

Love is dependent upon reciprocity. Those among us who have started with good matches must nonetheless build upon what we have with a lifetime commitment to doing whatever it takes to make it last. If any of this can be reducible to laws of love, I would be the first to share them. But I'm not a believer in iron-clad determinism. Love is one of life's anomalies, and perhaps it's best faced with bemused puzzlement rather than with professorial conceit. What I advise in general is to live an ethical life filled with purpose. I don't mean a life of sacrifice and sorrow, quite the opposite. The more joy and bliss, the better; it's the first rule of life. When the opportunity for enduring love then presents itself, embrace it with selfless devotion.

Proceeding with a strong moral compass that is built upon an unwavering sense of right and wrong is also essential to a life well lived. A commitment to following that path scrupulously is needed as well, especially when challenged. The highest moral challenge isn't acting ethically when the choice is apparent; it's acting ethically when it's not or when it's extraordinarily difficult to enact.

A strong moral compass is also a good conduit for finding like-minded matches. Though the probabilities of love may then increase, a corresponding willingness to dedicate oneself to it is crucial as well.

My goal throughout this book has been to reduce intractable problems to manageable assumptions, with the hope that some measure of truth will shine through. I persist because I believe this goal is noble, and I've been around long enough to have a decent chance of hitting the target every now and then. But only time will tell.

CONCLUSION

I'm a skeptical man, rarely impressed and often bored, all evident perhaps throughout this book. Though sex can be fantastic, research is another matter entirely. The passageway to meaningful data is narrow at best.

As I emphasized in Chapter 3, one of the few fundamental things I know about sex is that people lie like hell about it. Reproducibility of findings is dismal, too. Base-level statistical understanding is frequently scarce as well, but most problematic is the lack of rigor in measuring the phenomena we study. Psychological research makes for great sound bites, but the foundation upon which it rests is often irresolute.

What can a doubting Thomas or Thomasina do? I've chosen to look carefully at what I study and then describe it without fanfare. Acknowledging limitations is essential to my work. I've also, clearly, avoided repetition, preferring instead to emphasize exposition or theory, either narrative or mathematical, where fuzziness is less damning, or I've sought tangible precepts within the ambit of the law, where the issues are more circumscribed (e.g., a criminal offense) and corroboration (e.g., other witnesses, documentary pornography, a sexually transmitted disease) more likely. Both have also been salves for the tedium of academia (e.g., abortive committees, professorial posturing, and so on); the same is true for Crying 4 Kafka.

I believe that if you follow what fascinates you in an intellectually demanding way and work at it diligently, something meaningful will emerge. Now that I'm older and within striking distance of being wise, I've started writing about my life's work. Translating this knowledge into insight was the ultimate goal herein.

REFERENCES

Abramson, P. R. (1973). The relationship of the frequency of masturbation to several aspects of personality and behavior. *Journal of Sex Research, 9,* 132–142.

Abramson, P. R. (1977). Ethical requirements for research on human sexual behavior. *Journal of Social Issues, 33*, 184–192.

Abramson, P. R. (1984). *Sarah: A sexual biography*. Albany: SUNY Press.

Abramson, P. R. (1986). The cultural context of Japanese sexuality: An American perspective. *Psychologia: An International Journal of Psychology in the Orient, 29*, 1–9.

Abramson, P. R. (1988). Sexual assessment and the epidemiology of AIDS. *Journal of Sex Research, 25,* 323–346.

Abramson, P. R. (1990). Sexual science: Emerging discipline or oxymoron? *Journal of Sex Research, 27*, 147–165.

Abramson, P. R. (2007). *Romance in the Ivory Tower: The rights and liberty of conscience.* Cambridge, MA: MIT Press.

Abramson, P. R. (2010). *Sex appeal: Six ethical principles for the 21st century.* New York, NY: Oxford University Press.

Abramson, P. R. (2012). Brief of Amicus Curiae in support of Petitioner's Writ of Certiorari to the United States Supreme Court, Eric Leon Butt, Jr., v. Utah (pp. 1–23).

Abramson, P.R. (2017). *The Saint of Fucked-up Karma: A musical.* Joshua Tree, CA: Asylum 4 Renegades Press.

Abramson, P. R., & Abramson, A. (2014). Smells like teen spirit: The conundrum of kids, sex, and the law In S. Coupet & E. Marrus (Eds.), *Children, sex and the law* (pp. 6–29). New York: NYU Press.

Abramson, P. R., Boggs, R., & Mason, E. Jolie. (2013). Sex is blind: Some preliminary theoretical implications. *Sexuality and Disability, 31,*393–402.

Abramson, P. R., Cloud, M. Y., Keese, R., & Girardi, J. (1997). Proof positive: Pornography in a day-care center. *Sexual Abuse: A Journal of Research and Treatment, 9,* 75–87.

Abramson, P. R., Goldberg, P. A., Mosher, D. L., Abramson, L. M., & Gottesdiener, M. (1975). Experimenter effects on esponses to erotic stimuli. *Journal of Research in Personality, 9*, 136–146.

Abramson, P. R., Gross, T., & Abramson, A. B. (2012). Consenting to sex among individuals with severe mental illness: *Terra incognita* and a priest with AIDS. *Sexuality and Disability, 30,* 357–366.

Abramson, P. R., & Hayashi, H. (1984). Pornography in Japan. In N. M. Malamuth & E. Donnerstein (Eds.), *Pornography and sexual aggression* (pp. 104–125). New York, NY: Academic Press.

Abramson, P. R., & Mosher, D. L. (1975). The development of a measure of negative attitudes toward masturbation. *Journal of Consulting and Clinical Psychology, 43,* 485–490.

Abramson, P. R., & Mosher, D. L. (1979). An empirical investigation of experimentally induced masturbatory fantasies. *Archives of Sexual Behavior, 8,* 27–39.

Abramson, P. R., Parker, T., & Weisberg, S. (1988). Sexual expression of mentally retarded people: Educational and legal implications. *American Journal of Mental Retardation, 93,* 328–334.

Abramson, P. R., & Pearsall, E. H. (1983). Pectoral changes during the sexual response cycle: A thermographic analysis. *Archives of Sexual Behavior, 12,* 357–368.

Abramson, P. R., Perry, L. B., Rothblatt, A., Seeley, T. T., & Seeley, D. M. (1981). Negative attitudes toward masturbation and pelvic vasocongestion: A thermographic analysis. *Journal of Research in Personality, 15,* 497–509.

Abramson, P. R., Perry, L. B., Seeley, T. T., Seeley, D. M., & Rothblatt, A. (1981). Thermographic measurement of exual arousal. *Archives of Sexual Behavior, 10*, 171–176.

Abramson, P. R., & Pinkerton, S. D. (Eds.). (1995a). *Sexual nature/sexual culture.* Chicago, IL: University of Chicago Press.

Abramson, P. R., & Pinkerton, S. D. (1995b). *With pleasure: Thoughts on the nature of human sexuality.* New York, NY: Oxford University Press.

Abramson, P. R., & Pinkerton, S. D. (1996). Electrons and sex. *Science, 273,* 1155–1156.

Abramson, P. R., & Pinkerton, S. D. (1998). The handy-dandy kitchen device. *Science, 282,* 1993.

Abramson, P. R., & Pinkerton, S. D. (2001). *A house divided: Suspicions of mother–daughter incest.* New York, NY: Norton.

Abramson, P. R., & Pinkerton, S. D. (2005.) Sexual illiteracy. *American Sexuality Magazine, 3*(4), 1–7.

Abramson, P. R., Pinkerton, S .D., & Huppin, M. (2003). *Sexual rights in America: The Ninth Amendment and the pursuit of happiness.* New York: NYU Press.

Acton, W. (1957). *The functions and disorders of the reproductive organs.* London, England: Churchill.

198

Ainsworth, M. D. S. (1982). Attachment: Retrospect and
　　prospect. In C. M. Parkes & J. Stevenson-Hinde
　　(Eds.), *The place of attachment in human behavior*
　　(pp. 3–30). New York, NY: Basic Books.

Ainsworth, M. D. S. (1989). Attachments beyond infancy.
　　American Psychologist, 44, 709–716.

Ainsworth, M. D. S., & Bowlby, J. (1991). An ethological
　　approach to personality development. *American
　　Psychologist, 46,* 331–334.

Alonzo, S. H. (2015). An unexpected cost of sex: Coevolution of
　　male and female mosquitoes influences whether
　　mosquitoes transmit human malaria. *Science, 347,*
　　948-949.

Ashcroft v. Free Speech Coalition, 535 U.S. 234 (2002).

Attorney General Edwin Meese's Commission on Pornography.
　　(1986, July). *Final report: Attorney General Edwin Meese's
　　Commission on Pornography* (pp. 1650–1651).
　　Washington, DC: Government Printing Office.

Baggerly, K. A., & Coombes, K. R. (2009). Deriving
　　chemosensitivity from cell lines: Forensic bioinformatics
　　and reproducible research in high-thoughout biology.
　　Annals of Applied Statistics, 3, 1309–1334.

Bailey, J. M. (2003). *The man who would be queen: The science of gender-bending and transsexualism.* Washington, DC: Joseph Henry Press.

Bailey, J. M., & Zucker, K. J. (1995). Childhood sex-typed behavior and sexual orientation: A conceptual analysis and quantitative review. *Developmental Psychology, 31,* 43–55.

Bailyn, B. (1992). The ideological origins of the American Revolution. Cambridge, MA: Harvard University Press.

Bailyn, B. (2015). *Sometimes an art.* New York, NY: Knopf.

Baker, R. R., & Bellis, M. A. (1995). *Human sperm competition: Copulation, masturbation, and infidelity.* London, England: Chapman & Hall.

Balter, M., & Gibbons, A. (2015). Indo-European languages tied to herders. *Science, 347,* 814–815.

Bancroft, J. (Ed.). (2003). *Sexual development in childhood.* Bloomington: Indiana University Press.

Bancroft, J. (2009). *Human sexuality and its problems.* Edinburgh, Scotland: Elsevier.

Bancroft, J., Herbenick, D., & Reynolds, M. (2003). Masturbation as a marker of sexual development. In J. Bancroft (Ed.), *Sexual development in childhood* (pp. 27–43). Bloomington: Indiana University Press.

Barnett, R. E. (1989). James Madison's Ninth Amendment. In R. E. Barnett (Ed.), *The rights retained by the 66 Amendment: Vol. 1* (pp. 1–50). Fairfax, VA: George Mason University.

Barnett, R. E. (1993). Implementing the Ninth Amendment. In R. E. Barnett (Ed.), *The rights retained by the people: The history and meaning of the Ninth Amendment: Vol. 2* (pp. 1–46). Fairfax, VA: George Mason University.

Barrett, R. D. H., & Hoekstra, H. E. (2011). Molecular spandrels: Test of adaptations at the genetic level. *Nature Review Genetics, 12,* 767–780.

Beam, G. (2012). *The problem with survey research.* New Brunswick, NJ: Transaction.

Beer, L. W. (1984). *Freedom of expression in Japan: A study of comparative law, politics, and society.* Tokyo, Japan: Kodansha International.

Beerbohm, M. (1920). *And even now.* New York, NY: Dutton.

Bentler, P. M., & Abramson, P. R. (1981). The science of sex research: Some methodological considerations. *Archives of Sexual Behavior, 10,* 225–25l.

Berger, S .L., et al. (2009). An operational definition of epigenetics. *Genes & Development, 23,* 781–783.

Berk, R., Abramson, P. R., & Okami, P. (1995). Sexual activities as told in surveys. In P. R. Abramson & S. D. Pinkerton

(Eds.), *Sexual nature/sexual culture* (pp. 371–386). Chicago, IL: University of Chicago Press.

Berlin, I. (1969). *Four essays on liberty.* Oxford, England: Oxford University Press.

Berntson, G. G., & Cacioppo, J. T. (2000). From homeostasis to allodynamic regulation. In J. T. Cacioppo & G. G. Berntson (Eds.), *Handbook of psychphysiology* (2nd ed.) (pp. 459–481). New York, NY: Cambridge University Press.

Bethel School District v. Fraser, 478 U.S. 675 (1986).

Bloom, D. (1998). Technology, experimentation, and the quality of survey data. *Science, 280,* 847–848.

Blum, D. (2002). *Love at Goon Park: Harry Harlow and the science of affection.* New York, NY: Basic Books.

Bogart, L. M., Pinkerton, S. D., Cecil, H., Myaskovsky, L., Wagstaff, D. A., & Abramson, P. R. (1999). The meaning of sex. *Journal of the American Medical Association, 282,* 1917–1918.

Borges, J. L. (1975). *Other Inquisitions: 1937–1952.* Austin: University of Texas Press.

Boswell, J. (1994). Same-sex unions in premodern Europe. New York, NY: Vintage.

Bowers v. Hardwick, 478 U.S. 186 (1986).

Bowlby, J. (1969). *Attachment and loss: Vol. 1. Attachment.* New York, NY: Basic Books.

Bowlby, J. (1973). *Attachment and loss: Vol. 2. Separation.* New York, NY: Basic Books.

Bowlby, J. (1980). *Attachment and loss: Vol. 3. Loss, sadness, and depression.* New York, NY: Basic Books.

Brown, C. (2011). *Paying for it: A comic strip memoir about being a john.* Montreal, Canada: Drawn & Quarterly.

Buchman, T. G. (2002). The community of the self. *Nature, 420,* 246–251.

Buss, D. (1995). *The evolution of desire: Strategies of human mating.* New York, NY: Basic Books.

Cacciatore, R. (2000). Sexual health in children. In I. Lottes & O. Kontula (Eds.), *New views on sexual health: The case of Finland* (pp. 65–79). Vammala, Finland: Population Research Institute.

Cacioppo, J. T., et al. (2000). Multi-level integrative analyses of human behavior: Social neuroscience and the complementing nature of social and biological approaches. *Psychological Bulletin, 126,* 829–843. Cal. Pen. Code § 288a(g). Emphasis added.

Campas, O., Mallarino, R., Herrel, A., Abzhanov, A., & Brenner, M. P. (2010). Scaling and shear transformations capture beak shape variation in Darwin's finches. *Proceedings of the National Academy of Sciences, 107,* 3356–3360.

Carneiro, M., et al. (2011). The genetic structure of domestic rabbits. *Molecular Biology and Evolution, 28,* 1801–1816.

Carneiro, M., et al. (2014). Rabbit genome analysis reveals a polygenic basis for phenotypic change during domestication. *Science, 345,* 1074–1079.

Carpenter, S. (2012). Psychology's bold initiative. *Science, 335,* 1558.

Carrier, J. (1995). *De los otros: Intimacy and homosexuality among Mexican men.* New York, NY: Columbia University Press.

Case, M. A. (2010). Why feminists have to lose in same-sex marriage litigation. *UCLA Law Review, 57,* 1199–1233.

Chagnon, N. (1968) *Yanomano: The fierce people.* New York, NY: Holt McDougal.

Child Protection Act of 1984, Pub. L. No. 98-292, 98 Stat. 206.

Churchland, P. S. (2011). *Braintrust: What neuroscience tells us about morality.* Princeton, NJ: Princeton University Press.

Churchland, P. S., & Sejnowski, T.J. (1992). *The computational brain.* Cambridge, MA: MIT Press.

Coetzee, J. M. (1996). *Giving offense: Essays on censorship.* Chicago, IL: University of Chicago Press.

Cogan, N. H. (1997). *The complete Bill of Rights.* New York, NY: Oxford University Press.

Cohen, J. (2014). Early AIDS virus may have ridden Africa's rails. *Science, 346,* 21–23.

Cohen, M. R., & Nagel, E. (1934.) *An introduction to logic and the scientific method.* New York, NY: Harcourt, Brace.

Comte-Sponville, A. (2001). *A small treatise on the great virtues.* New York, NY: Metropolitan Books.

Conley, T. D. (2011). Perceived proposer personality characteristics and gender differences in acceptance of casual sex offers. *Journal of Personality and Social Psychology, 100,* 309–329.

Coupet, S., & Marrus, E. (Eds.). *Children, sex, & the law.* New York: NYU Press.

Crowne, D. P., & Marlowe, D. (1964). *The approval motive: Studies in evaluative dependence.* New York, NY: Wiley.

Currie, D. P. (1988). *The Constitution of the United States: A primer for the people.* Chicago, IL: University of Chicago Press.

Daly, M., & Wilson, M. (1988). Evolutionary social psychology and family homicide. *Science, 242,* 519–524.

Damrosch, L. (2015). *Eternity's sunrise: The imaginative world of William Blake.* New Haven, CT: Yale University Press.

Darwin, C. (1873). *The origin of the species.* London, England: Murray.

Dawson, J. W. (2006). *Logical dilemmas: The life and work of Kurt Godel.* Natick, MA: A .K. Peters.

DeLamater, J. D., & Friedrich, W. N. (2002). Human sexual development. *Journal of Sex Research, 39,* 10–14.

Des Jariais, D. C., Paone, D., Milliken, J., Turner, C. F., Miller, H., Gribble, J., . . . Friedman, S. R. (1999). Audio-computer interviewing to measure risk behavior for HIV among injecting drug users: A quasi-randomized trial. *Lancet, 353,* 1657–1661.

De Swaan, A. (2015). *The killing compartments: The mentality of mass murder.* New Haven, CT: Yale University Press.

Devries, K. M., et al. (2013). The global prevalence of intimate violence against women. *Science, 340,* 1527–1528.

de Waal, F. B. M. (1982). *Chimpanzee politics: Power and sex among apes.* Baltimore, MD: Johns Hopkins University Press.

de Waal, F. B. M. (1989). *Peacemaking among primates.* Cambridge, MA: Harvard University Press.

de Waal, F. B. M. (2001a) *The ape and the sushi maker.* New York, NY: Basic Books.

de Waal, F. B. M. (2001b). *Tree of origin: What primate behavior can tell us about human social evolution.* Cambridge, MA: Harvard University Press.

de Waal, F. B. M. (2005). *Our inner ape.* New York, NY: Penguin.

Diamond, J. (1997). *Why is sex fun?* New York, NY: Basic Books.

Diamond, J. (2005). *Collapse: How societies choose to fall or succeed.* New York, NY: Penguin.

Diamond, L. (2009). *Sexual fluidity: Understanding women's love and desire.* Cambridge, MA: Harvard University Press.

Doe v. Commonwealth's Attorney, 425 U.S. 901 (1976), *aff'g mem.* 403 F. Supp. 1100 (E.D. VA. 1975).

Donoso, M., Collins, A. G. E., & Koechlin, E. (2014). Foundations of human reasoning in the prefrontal cortex. *Science, 344,* 1481–1486.

Duberman, M. (1993). *Stonewall.* New York, NY: Penguin.

Dworkin, A. (1987a). *Ice and fire.* New York: Grove Weidenfeld.

Dworkin, A. (1987b). *Intercourse* (p. 12). New York, NY: Free Press.

Dworkin, A. (1993). *Letters from a war zone* (pp. 200–201). Chicago, IL: Lawrence Hill Books.

Dwokin, R. (1993). *Life's dominions.* New York, NY: Vintage.

Dyble, M., et al. (2015). Sex equality can explain the unique social structure of hunter-gatherer bands. *Science, 348,* 796–798.

Edwards, A. L. (1970). *The measurement in personality traits by scales and inventories.* New York, NY: Holt, Rinehart & Winston.

Eig, J. (2014). *The birth of the pill.* New York, NY: Norton.

Eiland, H., & Jennings, M. W. (2014). *Walter Benjamin: A critical life.* Cambridge, MA: Belknap Press of Harvard University Press.

Einstein, G. (2007). *Sex and the brain.* Cambridge, MA: MIT Press.

Eltahawy, M. (2015). *Headscarves and hymens: Why the Middle East needs a sexual revolution.* New York, NY: Farrar, Straus & Giroux.

Fausto-Sterling, A. (2000). *Sexing the body: Gender politics and the construction of sexuality.* New York, NY: Basic Books.

Feynman, R. P., Leighton, R. B., & Sands, M. (2011). *Feynman Lectures on Physics: The new millennium edition.* New York, NY: Basic Books.

Fine, C. (2010). *Delusions of gender: How our minds, society, and neurosexism create difference.* New York, NY: Norton.

Finkelhor, D., Williams, L. M., & Burns, N. (1988). *Nursery crimes: Sexual abuse in day care.* Newbury Park, CA: Sage.

Fisher, R. A. (1930). *The genetical theory of natural selection.* Oxford, England: Clarendon Press.

Fleischman, D. S., Fessler, D. M. T., & Cholakians, A. E. (in press). Testing the affiliation hypothesis of homoerotic motivation in humans: The effects of progesterone and priming. *Archives of Sexual Behavior.*

Foucault, M. (1980). *The history of sexuality.* New York, NY: Vintage.

Franco, A., Malhotra, N., & Simonovits, G. (2014). Publication bias in the social sciences: Unlocking the file drawer. *Science, 345,* 1502–1504.

Franklin, S. (2013). *Biological relatives: IVF, stem cells, and the future of kinship.* Durham, NC: Duke University Press.

Freeman, D. (1983). *Margaret Mead and Samoa: The making and unmaking of an anthropological myth.* Cambridge, MA: Harvard University Press.

French, C. (2012, March 15). Precognition studies and the curse of failed replications. *The Guardian*, p. 38.

Friedrich, W. N., Fisher, J., Broughton, D., Houston, M., & Shafran, C. R. (1998). Normative sexual behavior in children: A contemporary sample. *Pediatrics, 101,* E9.

Gagnon, J. H., & Simon, W. (1973). *Sexual conduct.* Chicago, IL: Aldine.

Galenson, E. (1990). Observation of early infantile sexual and erotic development. In M. E. Perry (Ed.), *Handbook of sexology: Vol. 7* (pp. 108–124). Amsterdam, The Netherlands: Elsevier.

Garcia-Berthou, E., & Alcaraz, C. (2004). Incongruence between test statistics and *p* values in medical papers. *BMC Medical Research Methodology, 4,* 13.

Garnett v. State, 632 A. 2d 797 (1993).

Gelman, A., & O'Rourke, K. (2014). Difficulties in making inferences about scientific truth from distributions of published *p* values. *Biostatistics, 15,* 18–22.

Gendron, C. M., et al. (2014). *Drosophila* life span and physiology are modulated by sexual perception and reward. *Science, 343,* 544–548.

Gibbons, A. (2014a). How we tamed ourselves—and became modern. *Science, 346,* 405–406.

Gibbons, A. (2014b). The thoroughly bred horse. *Science, 346,* 1439.

Glazer, E. M. (2008). When obscenity discriminates. *Northwestern University Law Review, 102,* 1379–1434.

Gleiser, M. (2014). *The island of knowledge: The limits of science and the search for meaning.* New York, NY: Basic Books.

Godbeer, R. (2001). *Sexual revolution in early America.* Baltimore, MD: Johns Hopkins University Press.

Godbeer, R. (2002). *Sexual revolution in early America.* Baltimore, MD: Johns Hopkins University Press.

Goldberg, P. A. (1968). Are women prejudiced against women? *Transactions, 5,* 28–30.

Goldberg, P. A., Gottesdiener, M., & Abramson, P. R. (1975). Another put-down of women? Perceived attractiveness as a function of support for the feminist movement. *Journal of Personality and Social Psychology, 32,* 113–115.

Goldey, K. L., & van Anders, S. M. (2012). Sexual thoughts: Links to testosterone and cortisol in men. *Archives of Sexual Behavior, 41,* 1461–1470.

Gould, S. J. (1977). *Ontogeny and phylogeny.* Cambridge, MA: Harvard University Press.

Gould, S. J. (1997). The exaptive excellence of spandrels as a term and prototype. *Proceedings of the National Academy of Science, 94,* 10750–10755.

Gould, S. J., & Lewontin, R. C. (1979). The spandrels of San Marco and the Paglossian paradigm. *Proceedings of the Royal Society of London, 205,* 581–598.

Graaf, H. de, & Rademakers, J. (2011). The psychological measurement of childhood sexual development in Western societies: methodological challenges. *Journal of Sex Research, 48,* 118–129.

Graziano, M. S. A. (2013). *Consciousness and the social brain.* New York, NY: Oxford University Press.

Green, R. (1992). *Sexual science and the law.* Cambridge, MA: Harvard University Press.

Greenawalt, K. (1995). *Private conscience and public reasons.* New York, NY: Oxford University Press.

Greenland, S. (2005). Multiple-bias modeling for analysis of observational data. *Journal of the Royal Statistical Society, A, 168,* 267–306.

Grimm, D. (2015). Dawn of the dog. *Science, 348,* 274–279.

Griswold v. Connecticut, 381 U.S. 479 (1965).

Gutmann, M. (2007). *Fixing men: Sex, birth control, and AIDS in Mexico.* Berkeley, CA: University of California Press.

Hacker, A. (2014, October 23). Who knows the American mind? *New York Review of Books,* pp. 27–30.

Haines, C. G. (1944). *The role of the Supreme Court in American government and politics, 1789–1835.* Berkeley: University of California Press.

Haldane, J. B. S. (1955). Population genetics. *New Biology, 18,* 34–51.

Halley, J. (1993). Reasoning about sodomy: Act and identity in and after Bowers v. Hardwick. *Virginia Law Review, 79,* 1721–1780.

Hamer, D. (1994). *The Science of desire: The search for the gay gene and the biology of behavior.* New York, NY: Simon & Schuster.

Hamer, D. H., et al. (1993). A linkage between DNA markers on the X chromosome and male sexual orientation. *Science, 261,* 321–327.

Hamilton, W. D. (1963). The evolution of altruistic behavior. *American Naturalist, 97,* 354–356.

Hamilton, W. D. (1964). The genetical evolution of social behavior. *Journal of Theoretical Biology, 7,* 1–16.

Hand, D. J. (2014). *The improbability principle: Why coincidences, miracles, and rare events happen every day.* New York, NY: *Scientific American*/Farrar, Straus and Giroux.

Harlow, H. (1958). The nature of love. *American Psychologist, 13,* 673–685.

Harlow, H., et al. (1965). Total social isolation in monkeys. *Proceedings of the National Academy of Sciences, 54*(1), 90–97.

Hazelwood School District et al. v. Kulmeier et al., 484 U.S. 260 (1988).

Heisenberg, W. (2007). *Physics and philosophy: The revolution in modern science.* New York, NY: Harper.

Herdt, G. (1981). *Guardians of the flute.* New York, NY: McGraw-Hill.

Herdt, G. (2006). *The Sambia: Ritual, sexuality, and change in Papua, New Guinea.* Belmont, CA: Wadsworth.

Herdt, G., & Boxer, A. (1996). *Children of horizon.* Boston, MA: Beacon Press.

Hines, M. (2009). Gonadal hormones and sexual differentation of human brain and behavior. In D. Pfaff, A. P. Arnold, S. E. Etgen, S. E. Fahrbach, & R. T. Rubin (Eds.), *Hormones, brain, and behavior* (2nd ed., pp. 80–97). New York, NY: Academic Press.

Holmes, E. A., Craske, M. G., & Graybiel, A. M. (2014). Psychological treatments: A call for mental health science. *Nature, 511,* 287–289.

Hoshii, I. (1987). *The world of sex: Vol. 4. Sex in ethics and law.* Woodchurch, England: Paul Norbury.

Hunter, N. D. (2004). Living with Lawrence. *Minnesota Law Review, 88,* 1103–1139.

Ignatieff, M. (1998.) *Isaiah Berlin: A life.* New York, NY: Owl Books.

Inhorn, M. C., Chavkin, W., & Navarro, J. (Eds.). (2014.) *Globalized fatherhood.* New York, NY: Berghahn.

In re Gault, 387 U.S. 1 (1967).

Institute of Education Sciences. (2000). *National postsecondary student aid study (NPSAS).* Washington, DC: U.S. Department of Education.

Ioannidis, J. (2005). Why most published research findings are false. *PLOS Medicine, 2,* 0696-0701.

Isaacson, W. (2014). *The innovators.* New York, NY: Simon & Schuster.

Israeli rape by fraud cases. (2010, October 7). Retrieved from http://www.volokh.com

Izawa, C., & Ohta, N. (2005). *Human learning and memory.* New York, NY: Psychology Press / Taylor and Francis.

Jansen, Y.-O. (2007). The right to freely have sex? Beyond biology: Reproductive rights and sexual self-determination. *Akron Law Review, 40,* 311–337.

Jefferson, T. (1984). *Writings.* New York, NY: Library of America.

Joel, D., & Tarrasch, R. (2010). The risk of a wrong conclusion: On testosterone and gender differences in risk aversion and career choice. *Proceedings of the National Academy of Sciences, 107*(5), E19.

Johnson, M. (2014). *Morality for humans: Ethical understanding from the perspective of cognitive science.* Chicago, IL: University of Chicago Press.

Karkazis, K., & Jordan-Young, R. (2015). Debating a testosterone "sex gap." *Science, 348,* 858–860.

Kemeny, J. G. (1959). *A philosopher looks at science.* Princeton, NJ: Van Nostrand.

Kipnis, L. (1996). *Bound and gagged*. New York, NY: Grove Press.

Kitcher, P. (1985). *Vaulting ambition: Sociobiology and the quest for human nature*. Cambridge, MA: MIT Press.

Koch, A. (1966). *Madison's "Advice to my country."* Princeton, NJ: Princeton University Press.

Koechlin, E., & Hyafil, A. (2007). Anterior prefrontal function and the limits of human decision-making. *Science, 318,* 594–598.

Koechlin, E., Ody, C., & Kouneiher, F. (2003). The architecture of cognitive control in the human prefrontal cortex. *Science, 302,* 1181–1185.

Konvitz, M. R. (1963). *Religious liberty and conscience*. New York, NY: Viking.

Kosunen, E. (2000.) Adolescent sexual health. In I. Lottes & O. Kontula (Eds.), *New views on sexual health: The case of Finland* (pp. 3–18). Vammala, Finland: Population Research Institute.

Kuhn, T. S. (1962). *The structure of scientific revolutions*. Chicago, IL: University of Chicago Press.

Kutchinsky, B. (1985). Pornography and its effects in Denmark and the United States. *Comparative Social Research, 8,* 1–15.

Lambert v. California, 355 U.S. 225 (1957).

Lande, R. (1979). Quantitative genetic analysis of multivariate evolution, applied to brain: Body size allometry. *Evolution, 33,* 402–416.

Lange, K. (1997). An approximate model of polygenic inheritance. *Genetics, 147,* 1423–1430.

Larsson, I., & Svedin, C. G. (2002). Sexual experiences in childhood: Young adults' recollections. *Archives of Sexual Behavior, 31,* 263–273.

Laumann, E. O., Gagnon, J., Michael, R. T., & Michaels, S. (1994). *The social organization of sexuality.* Chicago, IL: University of Chicago Press.

Lawrence v. Texas, 539 U.S. 558 (2003).

LeDoux, J. (2015). *Anxious: Using the brain to understand and treat fear and anxiety.* New York, NY: Viking.

Leek, J. T., & Peng, R. D. (2015). What is the question? *Science, 347,* 1314–1315.

Le Galliard, J.-F., Fitze, P., Ferriere, R., & Clobert, J. (2005). Sex ratio bias, male aggression, and population collapse in lizards. *Proceedings of the National Academy of Sciences, 102,* 18231–18236.

LeVay, S. (1993). *The sexual brain.* Cambridge, MA: MIT Press.

Lewontin, R. (2000.) *The triple helix.* Cambridge, MA: Harvard University Press.

Lieberman, D., Pillsworth, E. G., & Haselton, M. (2011). Kin affiliation across the ovulatory cycle: Females avoid father when fertile. *Psychological Science, 22,* 13–18.

Lightfoot-Klein, H. (1989). The sexual experience and marital adjustment of genitally circumcised and infibulated females in the Sudan. *Journal of Sex Research, 26,* 375–392.

Linnen, C. R., Poh, Y. P., Peterson, B. K., Barrett, R. D. H., Larson, J. G., Jensen, J. D., & Hoekstra, H. E. (2013). Adaptive evolution of multiple traits through multiple mutations at a single gene. *Science, 339,* 1312–1316.

Lithwick, D. (2013, August 7). Ken Cucinelli's sodomy obsession. *Slate,* pp. 212–213.

Locke, J. (1980). *Second treatise of government.* Indianapolis, IN: Hackett.

Locke, J. (1812). *Works.* London, England: W. Otridge and Sons.

Lohmueller, K. E. (2014). On the origin of Peter Rabbit. *Science, 345,* 1000–1001.

Lottes, I., & Kontula, O. (Eds.). (2000). *New views on sexual health: The case of Finland.* Helsinki, Finland: Population Research Institute.

Loving v. Virginia, 388 U.S. 1 (1967).

Lubet, S. (1998). *Expert testimony: A guide for expert witnesses and lawyers who examine them.* Notre Dame, IN: National Institute of Trial Advocacy.

Lukas, D., & Huehard, E. (2014). The evolution of infanticide by males in mammalian societies. *Science, 346,* 841–844.

MacKinnon, C. A. (1991). Pornography as defamation and discrimination. *Boston University Law Review, 71,* 793–808.

MacKinnon, C. A. (1993). *Only words.* Cambridge, MA: Harvard University Press.

Madison, J. (1987). *Notes on debates in the Federal Convention.* New York, NY: Norton. (Original work published 1840).

Madison, J. (1999). *Writings.* Washington, DC: Library of America.

Maduro, M. F., & Rothman, J. H. (2002). Making worm guts: The gene regulatory network of the *caenorhabditis elegans* endoderm. *Developmental Biology, 246,* 68–85.

Margolick, D. (2001). *"Strange Fruit": The biography of a song.* New York, NY: HarperCollins.

Martinez, G., Copen, C. E., &, Abma, J. U.S. Department of Health and Human Services. (2011). *Teenagers in the United States: Sexual activity, contraceptive use, and childbearing, 2006–2010. National survey of family growth* (Vital and

Health Statistics, Series 23, No. 31). Washington, DC: Government Printing Office.

Martinson, F. M. (1994). *The sexual life of children.* Westport, CT: Bergin and Garvey.

Masters, W. H., Johnson, V., & Kolodny, R. C. (1982). *Human sexuality.* Boston, MA: Little, Brown.

Mayr, E. (1963). *Animal species and evolution.* Cambridge, MA: Belknap Press of Harvard University Press.

McBrearty, S., & Brooks, A. (2000). The revolution that wasn't: A new interpretation of the origin of modern human behavior. *Journal of Human Evolution, 39,* 453–563.

McCarthy, M. M., Arnold, A. P., Ball, G. F., Blaustein, J. D., & DeVries, G. J. (2012). Sex differences in the brain: The not so inconvenient truth. *Journal of Neuroscience, 32,* 2241–2247.

McConnell, M. (1990). The origins and historical understanding of free exercise of religion. *Harvard Law Review, 103,* 1409–1517.

Mead, M. (1928). *Coming of age in Samoa.* New York, NY: Morrow.

Meehl, P. (1973). *Psychodiagnosis: Selected papers.* New York, NY: Norton.

Mercer, F., & Abramson, P. R. (2009). Masturbation. In R. A. Shweder (Ed.), *The child* (pp. 98–100). Chicago, IL: University of Chicago Press.

Mervis, J. (2014). Why null results rarely see the light of day. *Science, 345,* 992.

Meyer-Bahlburg, H. F. L. (1995). Psychoneuroendocrinology and sexual pleasure: An aspect of sexual orientation. In P. R. Abramson, & S. D. Pinkerton (Eds.), *Sexual nature/sexual culture* (pp. 135–153). Chicago, IL: University of Chicago Press.

Meyers, M. (Ed.). (1981). *The mind of the founder: Sources of political thought of James Madison.* Hanover, NH: United Press of New England.

Michaels, A. C. (1999). Constitutional innocence. *Harvard Law Review, 112,* 828–902.

Mill, J. S. (1978). *On liberty.* Indianapolis, IN: Hackett.

Miller, P. (1962). *Roger Williams: His contribution to the American tradition.* New York, NY: Atheneum.

Miller v. California, 413 U.S. 15 (1973).

Miranda v. Arizona, 384 U.S. 436 (1966).

Mitchell, S. N., et al. (2015). Evolution of sexual traits influencing vectorial capacity in anopheline mosquitoes. *Science, 347,* 985–988.

Montaigne, M. de, & Frane, D. M. (1948). *The complete essays of Montaigne.* Palo Alto, CA: Stanford University Press.

Moore, J., & Ali, R. (1984). Are dispersal and inbreeding avoidance related? *Animal Behavior, 32,* 94–112.

Morgan, E. S. (1967). *Roger Williams: The church and the state.* New York, NY: Norton.

Mosher, D. L. (1966). The development and multitrait-multimethod matrix analysis of three measures of three aspects of guilt. *Journal of Consulting Psychology, 30,* 5–29.

Mosher, D. L. (1968). Measurement of guilt in females by self-report inventories. *Journal of Consulting and Clinical Psychology, 32,* 690–695.

Mosher, D. L., & Abramson, P. R. (1977). Subjective sexual arousal to films of masturbation. *Journal of Consulting and Clinical Psychology, 45,* 796–807.

Mosher, D. L., & Cross, H. J. (1971). Sex guilt and premarital sexual experiences of college students. *Journal of Consulting and Clinical Psychology, 36,* 27–32.

Murstein, B. I. (1965). *The handbook of projective techniques.* New York, NY: Basic Books.

NAACP v. Alabama, 357 U.S. 449 (1958).

Nash, S., & Domjan, M. (1991). Learning to discriminate the sex of conspecifics in male Japanese quail (*Coturnix coturnix japonica*): Tests of "biological constraints." *Journal of Experimental Psychology: Animal Behavior Processes, 17,* 342–353.

National Health Statistics Reports. (2011, March 3). *Sexual behavior, sexual attraction, and sexual identity in the United States: Data from the 2006–2008 national health survey of family growth* (Report No. 36). Washington, DC: Government Printing Office.

Neier, A., & Rothman, D. J. (2015, December 17). Under lock & key: How long? *New York Review of Books,* p. 81.

Neimark, J. (2015). Line of attack: Christopher Korch is adding up the costs of contaminated cell lines. *Science, 347,* 938–940.

Nevins-Saunders, E. (2010). Incomprehensible crimes: Defendants with mental retardation charged with statutory rape. *New York University Law Review, 85,* 1067–1129.

New York v. Ferber, 458 U.S. 747 (1982).

Obergefell v. Hodges, 576 U.S. (2015).

O'Connor v. Donaldson, 422 U.S. 563 (1975).

Okami, P., Olmstead, R., & Abramson, P. R. (1997). Sexual experiences in early childhood: 18-year longitudinal data from the UCLA Family Lifestyles Project. *Journal of Sex Research, 34,* 339–347.

Okami, P., Olmstead, R., Abramson, P. R., & Pendleton, L. (1998). Early childhood exposure to parental nudity and scenes of parental sexuality ("primal scenes"): An 18-year longitudinal study of outcome. *Archives of Sexual Behavior, 27*, 361–384.

Olstead v. United States, 277 U.S. 438, 478 (1928).

O'Sullivan, L. F., & Meyer-Bahlburg, H. F. L. (2003). African American and Latina inner-city girls' reports of romantic and sexual development. *Journal of Social and Personal Relationships, 20*, 221–238.

Ozer, E. J., Best, S., Weiss, D. S., & Lipsey, T. (2003). Predictors of posttraumatic stress disorder in adults: A meta-analysis. *Psychological Bulletin, 129*(1), 52–73.

Ozer, E. J., & Weiss, D. S. (2004). Who develops posttraumatic stress disorder? *Current Directions in Psychological Science, 13*(4), 169–172.

Paabo, S. (2014). *Neanderthal man: In search of lost genomes.* New York, NY: Basic Books.

Paine, T. (1987). *The Thomas Paine reader.* New York, NY: Penguin. (Original work published 1776).

Palumbi, S. R., et al. (2014). Mechanisms of reef coral resistance to future climate change. *Science, 344*, 895–898.

Parenti, L. R., & Ebach, M. C. (2009). *Comparative biogeography.* Berkeley: University of California Press.

Parker, T. A., & Abramson, P. R. (1995). The law hath not been dead: Protecting adults with developmental disabilities from sexual abuse and violation of their sexual freedom. *Mental Retardation, 33*, 257–263.

Pattatucci, A. M. L., & Hamer, D. (1995). The genetics of sexual orientation: From fruit flies to humans. In P. R. Abramson & S. D. Pinkerton, (Eds.), *Sexual nature/sexual culture* (pp. 154–176). Chicago, IL: University of Chicago Press.

Penley, C. (1997). *Nasa/Trek.* New York, NY: Verso.

Pennisi, E. (2013a). Evolution heresy? Epigenetics underlies heritable plant traits. *Science, 341,* 1055.

Pennisi, E. (2013b). Field test shows selection works in mysterious ways. *Science, 341,* 118.

People v. Giardino, 82 Cal. App. 4th 454, 462 (2000).

People v. Griffin, 117 Cal. 583, 585 (1897).

People v. Lewis, 75 Cal. App. 3d 513, 519 (1977).

People v. Mobley, 72 Cal. App. 4th 761, 788 (1999).

People v. Thompson, 142 Cal. App. 4th 1426, 1434 (2006).

Perlin, M. L., and Cucolo, H.E. (2015). *Mental disability law: Civil and criminal* (3rd ed.). Newark, NJ: Lexis/Nexis Press.

Pfaff, D. W. (2014). *The altruistic brain: How we are naturally good.* New York, NY: Oxford University Press.

Pinkerton, S. D., & Abramson, P. R. (1992). Base rates revisited: Assessment strategies for HIV/AIDS. *Journal of Sex Research, 29*, 407–424.

Pinkerton, S. D., & Abramson, P. R. (1997). Homosexuality in Japan: Legal and social constraints. In D. J. West & R. Green (Eds.), *Sociolegal control of homosexuality: A multi-nation comparison* (pp. 106–152). New York, NY: Plenum.

Pinkerton, S. D., Cecil, H., Bogart, L. M., & Abramson, P. R. (2003). The pleasures of sex: An empirical investigation. *Cognition and Emotion, 17*, 341–353.

Planned Parenthood of Southeastern Pennsylvania v. Casey, 505 U.S. 833 (1992).

People v. Thompson, 142 Cal. App. 4th at 1437 (2006).

Popper, K. (1956). *Realism and the aim of science.* Totowa, NJ: Rowman & Littlefield.

Popper, K. (1957). *The Poverty of historicism.* London, England: Ark.

Popper, K. (1962). *The open society and its enemies* (Vols. 1–2). Princeton, NJ: Princeton University Press.

Popper, K. (1972). *Objective knowledge: An evolutionary approach.* New York, NY: Oxford University Press.

Posner, R. A. (1992). *Sex and reason.* Cambridge, MA: Harvard University Press.

226

Posner, R. A., & Silbaugh, K. B. (1996). *A guide to America's sex laws.* Chicago, IL: University of Chicago Press.

Prager, J. A. (2016, December2). Chilling photograph's hidden history. *The Wall Street Journal,* p. 39.

Promislow, D. E. L., & Kaeberlein, M. (2014). Chemical warfare in the battle of the sexes. *Science, 343,* 491–492.

Qiu, J. (2015). Dinosaur climate probed. *Science, 348,* 1185.

Ramsey, C. B., et al. (2012). A complete terrestrial radiocarbon record for 11.2 to 52.8 kyr B.P. *Science, 33,* 370–374.

Rawls, J. (1971). *A theory of justice.* Cambridge, MA: Harvard University Press.

Reed, J. (1978). *From private vice to public virtue.* New York, NY: Basic Books.

Reynolds, M. A., Herbenick, D. L., & Bancroft, J. H. (2003). The nature of childhood sexual experiences: Two studies 50 years apart. In J. Bancroft (Ed.), *Sexual development in childhood* (pp. 89–104). Bloomington, IN: Indiana University Press.

Rhode, D. L. (2016). *Adultery: Infidelity and the law.* Cambridge, MA: Harvard University Press.

Richards, D. A. J. (1974). Free speech and obscenity law: Toward a moral theory of the First Amendment. *University of Pennsylvania Law Review, 123,* 45–91.

Richards, D. A. J. (2009). *The sodomy cases: Bowers v. Hardwick and Lawrence v. Texas.* Lawrence: University Press of Kansas.

Richardson, S. S. (2013). *Sex itself: The search for male and female in the human genome.* Chicago, IL: University of Chicago Press.

Richelle L. v. Roman Catholic Archbishop, 106 Cal. App. 4th 257, 272 (2004).

Rilling, J. K. (2013). The neural and hormonal bases of human parental care. *Neuropsychologia, 51,* 731–747.

Robinson, P. (1977). *The modernization of sex: Havelock Ellis, Alfred Kinsey, William Masters and Virginia Johnson.* New York: Harper's.

Robinson, P. (1999). *Gay lives.* Chicago, IL: University of Chicago Press.

Robinson, P. (2005). *Queer wars.* Chicago, IL: University of Chicago Press.

Roe v. Wade, 410 U.S. 113 (1973).

Rosenbury, L. A., & Rothman, J. E. (2010). Sex in and out of intimacy. *Emory Law Journal, 59,* 809–868.

Rosenthal, R., & Rosnow, R. L. (2009). *Artifacts in behavioral research.* New York, NY: Oxford University Press.

Rosewarne, L. (2014). *Masturbation in pop culture, screen, society, and self.* Washington, DC: Rowman & Littlefield.

Ross, C. (2015). *Lessons in censorship: How schools and courts subvert students' First Amendment rights.* Cambridge, MA: Harvard University Press.

Rothman, D. J. (1971). *The discovery of the asylum: Social order and disorder in the new republic.* New York, NY: Little, Brown.

Rothman, D. J. (1980). *Conscience and convenience: The asylum and its alternatives in progressive America.* New York, NY: Little, Brown.

Rotter, J. B., Chance, J. E., & Phares, E. J. (1972). *Applications of a social learning theory of personality.* New York, NY: Holt, Rinehart & Winston.

Rousseau, J. J. (1992). *Discourse on the sciences and arts and polemics.* Hanover, NH: Dartmouth Press.

Ruths, D., & Pfeffer, J. (2014). Social media for large studies of behavior. *Science, 346,* 1063–1064.

Ryle, G. (1949). *The concept of mind.* Chicago, IL: University of Chicago Press.

Saks, E. (1990–1991). Competency to refuse treatment. *North Carolina Law Review,69,* 946–999.

Saks, E. (2002). *Refusing care: Forced treatment and the rights of the mentally ill.* Chicago, IL: University of Chicago Press.

Salmon, S., & Symons, D. (2001). *Warrior lovers: Erotic fiction, evolution, and female sexuality*. London, England: Weidenfield & Nicolson.

Scheffer, M., & Carpenter, S. R. (2003). Catastrophic regime shifts in ecosystems: Linking theory to observation. *Trends in Ecology and Evolution, 18,* 648–656.

Scheffer, M., Carpenter, S., Foley, J. A., Folke, C., & Walker, B. (2001). Catastrophic shifts in ecosystems. *Nature, 413,* 591–596.

Schuhrke, B. (2000). Young children's curiosity about other people's genitals. *Journal of Psychology & Human Sexuality, 12,* 27–48.

Sedgwick, E. K. (1990). *Epistemology of the closet.* Berkeley: University of California Press.

Seeley, T. T., Abramson, P. R., Perry, L. B., Rothblatt, A., & Seeley, D. M. (1980). Thermographic measurement of sexual arousal: A methodological note. *Archives of Sexual Behavior, 9,* 77–85.

Segerstrale, U. (2013). *Nature's oracle: The life and work of W. D. Hamilton.* Oxford, England: Oxford University Press.

Service, R. F. (2015). Signs of ancient proteins seen inside dinosaur bones. *Science, 348,* 1184.

Servick, K. (2014). New support for the gay gene. *Science, 346,* 902.

Shi, C., & Murphy, C. T. (2014). Mating induces shrinking and death in *caenorhabitis* mothers. *Science, 343,* 536–540.

Shipp, P. A. (Ed.). (1974). *The philosophy of Karl Popper* (Vols. 1–2). LaSalle, IL: Open Court Press.

Simic, C. (2015). *The life of images: Selected prose.* New York, NY: HarperCollins.

Sisti, D. A., Segal, A. G., and Emanuel, E. J. (2015). Improving long-term psychiatric care: Bring back the asylum. *JAMA, 313*(3), 1757.

Smith, J. M. (1995). *The Republic of letters: The correspondence between Jefferson and Madison.* New York: Norton.

Soria-Carrasco, V., et al. (2014). Stick insect genomes reveal natural selection's role in parallel speciation. *Science, 334,* 738–742.

Stangneth, B. (2014). *Eichmann before Jerusalem.* New York, NY: Knopf.

Stanley v. Georgia, 394 U.S. 557 (1969).

Stein, M. (2010). *Sexual injustice.* Chapel Hill: University of North Carolina Press.

Sterngold, James. (1996, December 3). Judge throws out Keating's verdict. *The New York Times*, pp. 29–30.

Strahilevitz, L. (2005). Consent, aesthetics, and the boundaries of sexual privacy after *Lawrence. DePaul Law Review, 54,* 671–701.

Strasak, A. M., et al. (2007). The use of statistics in medical research. *American Statistician, 61,* 47–55.

Suddendorf, T. (2013). *The gap: The science of what separates us from other animals.* New York, NY: Basic Books.

Sweezy v. New Hampshire, 354 U.S. 234 (1957).

Symons, D. (1979). *The evolution of human sexuality.* New York, NY: Oxford University Press.

Symons, D. (1992). On the use and misuse of Darwinism in the study of human behavior. In J. H. Barlow, L. Cosmides, & J. Tooby (Eds.), *The adapted mind: Evolutionary psychology and the generation of culture* (pp. 137–159). New York, NY: Oxford University Press.

Symons, D. (1995.) Beauty is in the adaptation of the behavior: The evolutionary psychology of human female sexual attractiveness. In P. R. Abramson & S. D. Pinkerton (Eds.), *Sexual nature/sexual culture* (pp. 80–120). Chicago, IL: University of Chicago Press.

Talhelm, T., et al. (2014). Large-scale psychological differences within China explained by rice versus wheat agriculture. *Science, 344,* 603–608.

Tannenhaus, D. S. (2011). *The constitutional rights of children: In re Gault and juvenile justice.* Lawrence: University Press of Kansas.

Tattersall, I. (2015). *The strange case of Rickety Cossack: And other cautionary tales from human evolution.* New York, NY: Palgrave Macmillan.

Texas GOP: Ban Sodomy. (2010, June 21). Wingnuts. *The Daily Beast.* http://www.thedailybeast.com/cheat-sheet/item/texas-gop-ban-sodomy/wingnuts/#

Thomas, K. (1992). Beyond the privacy principle. *Columbia Law Review, 92,* 1431–1516.

Thompson, J. N. (2013). *Relentless evolution.* Chicago, IL: University of Chicago Press.

Thornhill, R., & Palmer, C. T. (2000). *A natural history of rape: Biological bases of sexual coersion.* Cambridge, MA: MIT Press.

Tinker v. Des Moines Independent Community School District, 393 U.S. 503 (1969).

Tribe, L. H. (2004). *Lawrence v. Texas:* The "fundamental right" that dare not speak its name. *Harvard Law Review, 117,* 1893–1955.

Trivers, R. L. (1971). The evolution of reciprocal altruism. *Quarterly Review of Biology, 46,* 35–57.

Trivers, R. L. (1972). Parental investment and sexual selection. In B. Campbell (Ed.), *Sexual selection and the descent of man* (pp. 136–207). Chicago, IL: Aldine.

Trivers, R. L. (2011). *The folly of fools: The logic of deceit and self-deception in human life.* New York, NY: Basic Books.

Turner, C., et al. (1998). Adolescent sexual behavior, drug use, and violence: Increased reporting with computer survey technology. *Science, 280,* 867–873.

UNICEF. The Convention for the Rights of the Child. (2011). http://www.unicef.org/crc/index_30229.html

United States v. Dost, 636 F. Supp. 828, 833 (S.D. Cal. 1986).

United States v. S. A. Knox, 32 F. 733 (3rd Cir. 1994).

United States v. Roth 354 U.S. 476 (1957).

Urbach, P. (1987). *Francis Bacon's philosophy of science.* LaSalle, IL: Open Court.

Venn, O., et al. (2014). Strong male bias drives germline mutation in chimpanzees. *Science, 344,* 1272–1275.

Wade, L. (2014). Friends, not foes, boost warriors' success. *Science, 346,* 535.

Wagstaff, D. A., Abramson, P. R., & Pinkerton, S. D. (2000). Research in human sexuality. In L. T. Szuchman & F. Muscarella (Eds.), *Psychological perspectives on human sexuality* (pp. 3–59) . New York, NY: Wiley.

Wain, J. (Ed.). (1994). *The journals of James Boswell: 1762–1795.* New Haven, CT: Yale University Press.

Waites, M. (2005). *The age of consent: Young people, sexuality, and citizenship.* Hampshire, England: Palgrave Macmillan.

POLYCYSTIC LIVER DISEASE: INFORMATION FOR PATIENTS

When the daughter of medical journalist David Drum was diagnosed with polycystic liver disease, he found little information to help his daughter. After doing extensive medical research, Drum gathered the information he collected into a book to help other people understand this rare liver disease.

Polycystic Liver Disease: Information for Patients explains the development of polycystic liver disease, the important role of the liver in the body, how liver cysts form, and highlights the most common symptoms including the symptom of pain. Included is pertinent information on diet, herbs, and lifestyle choices for people living with the disease.

This print edition surveys the five major surgeries and surgical procedures doctors use to treat symptomatic polycystic liver disease and lays out the benefits, drawbacks, and possible complications of each. It looks at useful drugs still in clinical trials, and new treatments like hepatic artery embolion. The book also includes an explanation of the many liver function tests employed by doctors, links to useful web sites, a glossary, and a bibliography of sources.

DAVID DRUM is a medical journalist and the author or co-author of seven books in the health and wellness area. His books include *The Chronic Pain Management Sourcebook*, *Making the Chemotherapy Decision*, and *What Your Doctor Might NOT Tell you about Uterine Fibroids*, co-written with Scott Goodwin, MD, and Michael Broder, MD.

ISBN 9780991185764

90000

9 780991 185764

COCONUT
TOP TEN

This book explores the benefits of coconuts as a healthy addition to any diet, as an ingredient in healthcare products for hair and skin, and in a variety of other uses. The book begins with the origin of the coconut. It goes on to provide scientifically based facts that explain why coconuts are helpful in reducing belly fat, stretch marks, and wrinkles, among other health benefits. Among the more surprising tidbits are descriptions of the utilization of the coconut in warfare, rituals, and art. The book also includes dozens of coconut-based recipes for appetizers, entrees, drinks, and desserts. Its top-ten format makes it easy to read and valuable as a reference book. *Coconut Top Ten* is a treasure trove for coconut lovers and those interested in learning about this most versatile of superfoods.

Morgan H. Bishop is a seasoned freelance writer. In this book, he has combined meticulously researched facts with humor and top-ten lists, making for an easy and edifying read.

Red Scorpion Press

ISBN 9780998576855

9 780998 576855

90000 >

Wallace, B. (1991). Coadaptation revisited. *Journal of Heredity, 82,* 89–96.

Ward, J. L., & Blum, M. J. (2012). Exposure to an environmental estrogen breaks down sexual isolation between native and invasive species. *Evolutionary Applications, 5,* 901–912.

Watergate Trial Conversation Transcripts. (1973, April 16). Dean resignation conversation (p. 6). Yorba Linda, CA: Richard M. Nixon Presidential Library.

Waterman, J., Kelly, R. J., Oliveri, M. K., & McCord, J. (1993). *Behind the playground walls: Sexual abuse in preschools.* New York, NY: Guilford Press.

Weeks, J. (1985). *Sexuality and its discontents.* London, England: Routledge.

Werth, B. (2001). *The scarlet professor: Newton Arvin: A literary life shattered in scandal.* New York, NY: Anchor Books.

Wertheimer, A. (2003). *Consent to sexual relations.* Cambridge, England: Cambridge University Press.

Widom, C. S., Czaja, S. J., & DuMont, K. A. (2015). Intergenerational transmission of child abuse and neglect: Real or detection bias. *Science, 347,* 1480–1484.

Wiggins, J. (1973). *Personality and prediction: Principles of personality assessment.* Reading, MA: Addison-Wesley.

Wijgert, J. van de, Padian, N., Shiboski, S., & Turner, C. (2000). Is audio computer assisted self-interviewing a feasible method of surveying in Zimbabwe? *International Journal of Epidemiology, 29,* 885–890.

Williams, G. C. (1966). *Adaptation and natural selection.* Princeton, NJ: Princeton University Press.

Wills, G. (1978). *Inventing America.* New York, NY: Vintage.

Wilson, J. (1995). Sex hormones and sexual behavior. In P. R. Abramson & S. D. Pinkerton (Eds.), *Sexual nature/Sexual culture* (pp. 121–134). Chicago, IL: University of Chicago Press.

Wilson, M. L., et al. (2014). Lethal aggression in *Pan* is better explained by adaptive strategies than human impacts. *Nature, 513,* 414–417.

Wiser, M. J., Ribeck, N., & Lenski, R. E. (2013). Long-term dynamics of adaptation in asexual populations. *Science, 342,* 1364–1367.

Wright, S. (1922). Coefficients of inbreeding and relationship. *American Naturalist, 58,* 330–338.

Young, E. (2013). Psychologists strike a blow for reproducibility. *Nature, 503,* 403–412.

Zaretsky, R. (2015). *Boswell's enlightenment.* Cambridge, MA: Belknap Press of Harvard University Press.

the author

www.ingramcontent.com/pod-product-compliance
Lightning Source LLC
Chambersburg PA
CBHW060449280326
41933CB00014B/2707